THE COMPLETE MUSICIAN

THE COMPLETE MUSICIAN

STUDENT WORKBOOK, VOLUME I

An Integrated Approach to Tonal
Theory, Analysis, and Listening

Steven G. Laitz
The Eastman School of Music

New York   Oxford
OXFORD UNIVERSITY PRESS
2003

Oxford University Press

Oxford   New York
Auckland   Bangkok   Buenos Aires   Cape Town   Chennai
Dar es Salaam   Delhi   Hong Kong   Istanbul   Karachi   Kolkata
Kuala Lumpur   Madrid   Melbourne   Mexico City   Mumbai
Nairobi   São Paulo   Shanghai   Taipei   Tokyo   Toronto

Published by Oxford University Press, Inc.
198 Madison Avenue, New York, New York 10016
http://www.oup-usa.org

Oxford is a registered trademark of Oxford University Press

ISBN 0-19-5160592

Printing number: 9 8 7 6 5 4 3 2 1

Printed in the United States of America
on acid-free paper

CONTENTS

THE COMPLETE MUSICIAN

Tonality, The Musical Center

EXERCISE 1.1 Singing Scales

In a comfortable register, be able to sing a one-octave major scale or any of the three forms of the minor scale beginning on any pitch in both ascending and descending forms. Use scale degrees or solfège.

EXERCISE 1.2 Singing Scale Degrees

A. Play 1̂ in any major or minor key. Sing it, then be able to sing any other scale degree(s) in that key above or below it. In the beginning, you may find it easier to sing to the required scale degree by singing the scalar pitches between it and 1̂. For example, given the scale of E natural minor and 1̂ and the instruction to sing 5̂, you would sing 1̂–2̂–3̂–4̂ and then 5̂.

B. Starting on 3̂ or 5̂, be able to sing to any other scale degrees.

EXERCISE 1.3 Scale Practice: Error Detection

Below are misspelled scales; correct the errors by adding the appropriate accidentals and/or pitches. Examples A–C should be in the major mode, and D–F are in the minor mode. Assume that the tonic pitch is correct in all examples.

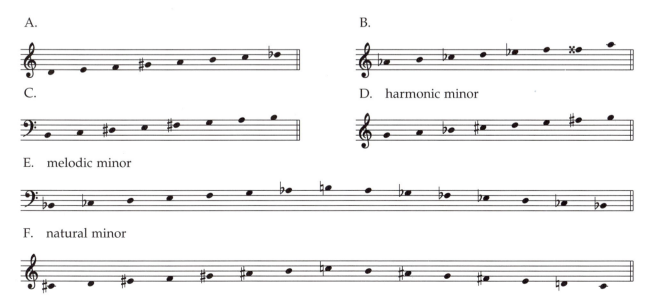

A.

B.

C.

D. harmonic minor

E. melodic minor

F. natural minor

EXERCISE 1.4   Key Signatures, Relative and Parallel Keys

A. Write the following key signatures from memory: A major, E♭ major, D minor, B major, G minor, F♯ minor, B♭ minor.

B. Name the relative minor keys of E♭ major, A♭ major, B major, and F major, then write their scales using accidentals, not key signatures.

C. Name the relative majors of C minor, F minor, G minor, and A♭ minor, then write their scales using accidentals, not key signatures.

D. Name the parallel minors of A, B, F♯, D, E♭, then write their scales using accidentals, not key signatures.

EXERCISE 1.5   Writing Scale Fragments

Study each scale fragment below and determine in which scales the fragments could be members; write out the complete scales and include scale degrees. For example, given the fragment A and B♭ and the instruction to list the major scales to which the pitches belong, the answer would be F major and B♭ major.

A. In which *major* scales are the following fragments members? List as many scales as would fit each fragment; there may only be a single solution or there may be multiple solutions.

D–E
F♯
A–B
D–E♭
B♭–D
G–C♯
F–A♭

B. In which *minor* scales are the following fragments members (all three forms of minor are possible)? Specify the form of minor.

D–E
A♭–C
A♭–B
F♯–G♯
B–F
F–A
C♯–F

C. In which *major and minor* scales are the following fragments members? Specify the form of minor.

E♭–F–G
F♯–G
C–E
G–D
A–B–C
F–G–A♭
E–B♭

EXERCISE 1.6   Scale Analysis: Minor Keys

Determine the minor scale/key by considering the following: the key signature for minor scales is derived from the natural minor scale; composers must raise $\hat{7}$ in order to create a half step between it and $\hat{8}$, the tonic. Thus, you will encounter an added sharp when the key signature contains sharps or an added natural when the key signature contains flats. For example, in E minor, the relative minor of G major, F♯, appears in the key signature. You will also encounter the accidental D♯, rather than D♮ on 7̂, since composers usually use a leading tone. One of the examples ends on its tonic; which one is it?

A. Schumann, "Hör ich das Liedchen klingen" ("When I Hear the Little Song"), *Dichterliebe*, op. 48

B. Schumann, "Wilder Reiter," *Album für die Jugend*, op. 68, no. 8

C. Schumann, "Es leuchtet meine Liebe" ("My Love Gleams"), op. 127, no. 3

D. Mozart, *Allegro molto*, Symphony No. 40 in G minor, K. 550

EXERCISE 1.7　Brain Twister

Below is a series of sharps and flats that will become key signatures. Notate these correctly on staff paper. Then, write the following required scales, which bear no relation to, and often contradict, the given key signatures. Notate the required scales using appropriate accidentals. For example, given the key signature of two sharps (i.e., F♯ and C♯), write a B♭ major scale. You would notate: B♭, C♮, D, E♭, F♮, G, A, B♭. Given the following key signatures of:

A. One sharp, write an E♭ major scale.
B. Three flats, write a D major scale.
C. Three sharps, write a C natural minor scale.
D. Four flats, write a C♯ harmonic minor scale.

EXERCISE 1.8　Melodic Dictation

Notate scale degrees for the major-mode melodic fragments.

A. ____ ____ ____ ____ ____
B. ____ ____ ____ ____ ____
C. ____ ____ ____ ____ ____ ____
D. ____ ____ ____ ____ ____ ____
E. ____ ____ ____ ____ ____ ____ ____
F. ____ ____ ____ ____ ____

EXERCISE 1.9   Melodic Dictation

Notate scale degrees for the minor-mode fragments.

A. ____ ____ ____ ____ ____
B. ____ ____ ____ ____ ____ ____ ____
C. ____ ____ ____ ____ ____ ____ ____
D. ____ ____ ____ ____ ____
E. ____ ____ ____ ____ ____ ____ ____
F. ____ ____ ____ ____ ____ ____ ____

EXERCISE 1.10   Melodic Dictation

Notate scale degrees of the minor-mode melodies.

A. ____ ____ ____ ____ ____ ____
B. ____ ____ ____ ____ ____ ____
C. ____ ____ ____ ____ ____
D. ____ ____ ____ ____ ____
E. ____ ____ ____ ____
F. ____ ____ ____ ____ ____ ____ ____

EXERCISE 1.11   Melodic Dictation

Notate scale degrees of the major- and minor-mode melodies that are played in different keys.

A. ____ ____ ____ ____ ____ ____ ____
B. ____ ____ ____ ____ ____
C. ____ ____ ____ ____ ____ ____ ____
D. ____ ____ ____ ____ ____ ____ ____
E. ____ ____ ____ ____ ____ ____ ____
F. ____ ____ ____ ____ ____ ____ ____

EXERCISE 1.12   Keyboard: Identification of Pitches

Using alternating hands, find and play all of the Gs on the keyboard. Begin by locating middle C and identifying all the Gs, first by descending in octaves and then by ascending. Continue this exercise in the same manner with the following pitch classes: D, C♯, A, F♯, B, E, C, B♭, E♭, F, and A.

EXERCISE 1.13   Keyboard: Matching Pitches

Play the following pitches on the keyboard and then sing each pitch. Begin by playing the pitches in the middle of the piano, then branch out and play pitches in other registers (that is, in different octaves above and below the original octave). When you sing these pitches, you will need to find a comfortable register.

A F B E♭ G C♯ C A♭ D F♯ B♭ E

EXERCISE 1.14   Keyboard: Bass and Treble Reading

Follow the instructions for Exercise 1.13. Ledger lines appear in this exercise: these are additional staff lines for notes above or below the regular five-line staff.

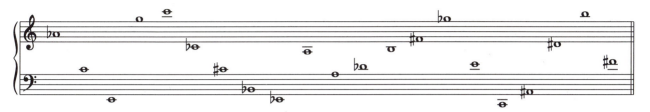

EXERCISE 1.15   Keyboard: Half and Whole Steps

Be able to play half and whole steps above and below the following pitches: D, G, F, B, A♭, E♭, B, C♯. Then, give yourself the starting pitch and sing half and whole steps above and below those pitches. In order to become fluent with this task and to sing in tune, view the given pitch as a scale degree within a key. For example, to sing a half step above D, consider D to be $\hat{7}$, and resolve this leading tone to $\hat{8}$, which is E♭. Similarly, in order to sing a whole step below D, consider D to be $\hat{2}$ in C major and then fall to $\hat{1}$, or C.

EXERCISE 1.16   Keyboard: Scales

Since scales have eight notes (seven different pitches and an octave duplication of the first pitch) and we have four fingers and one thumb on each hand, there is an easy method of playing scales: use the four fingers of your left hand beginning with the smallest finger, or "pinky" (finger numbers 5–4–3–2), to play the first four notes of a scale (referred to as the first tetrachord). Use the four fingers of your right hand to play the next four notes of the scale beginning with the index finger (finger numbers 2–3–4–5). Below is an illustration in D major:

	D	E	F♯	G		A	B	C♯	D
LH:	5	4	3	2	RH:	2	3	4	5

Play each scale in ascending and descending forms. Sing as you play. Play the major and three forms of minor scales (natural, harmonic, and melodic) in keys through two sharps and two flats. Try playing two notes, then singing the next two, playing the following two, and so on. Also, be able to jump immediately to any scale degree in a scale.

EXERCISE 1.17   Keyboard: Playing Major Scales Derived from Non-tonic Pitches

Construct the major scale derived from the scale degree function of the given pitch. For example, given the pitch G and $\hat{5}$, you count down five scale degrees to C and then play a C major scale.

given pitch:	C	F♯	A	B♭	E	B	D	C♯	B
given scale degree:	$\hat{4}$	$\hat{3}$	$\hat{7}$	$\hat{4}$	$\hat{3}$	$\hat{3}$	$\hat{3}$	$\hat{7}$	$\hat{3}$

EXERCISE 1.18   Keyboard: Playing Melodic Minor Scales from Nontonic Pitches

Follow the instructions for Exercise 1.17 above, but now the focus is on minor scales.

given pitch:	A	D	F	B♭	B♭	F♯	B	G	D
given scale degree:	$\hat{4}$	$\hat{3}$	$\hat{3}$	$\hat{3}$	$\hat{6}$	$\hat{5}$	$\hat{2}$	$\hat{3}$	$\hat{5}$
					(descending form)				

EXERCISE 1.19   Keyboard Scale Fragments

A. Given the following two- or three-note scale fragments, play the major scale(s) of which they are members. Hint: Remember that half steps occur both between $\hat{3}$ and $\hat{4}$ and between $\hat{7}$ and $\hat{8}$.

B. In the following example, you are given two-note scale fragments. Play the minor scale(s) of which they are the members.

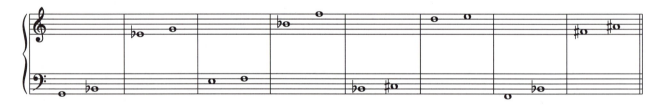

CHAPTER 2

Pulse, Rhythm, and Meter

EXERCISE 2.1 Matching

Each rhythm in column A may be matched with one or more different rhythms with the same total duration in column B. The first example in column A is completed for you.

EXERCISE 2.2 Matching

Match a rhythm from column A with one in column B that has the same total duration. Ties and rests are included. There may be more than one correct answer. The first example in column A is completed for you.

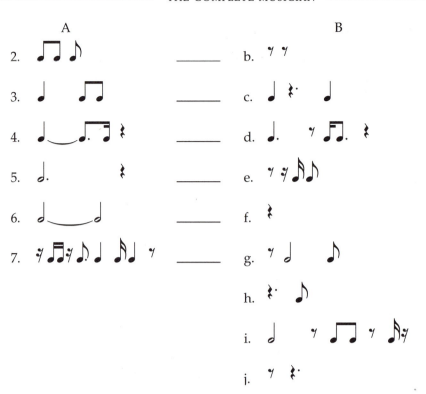

A   B

EXERCISE 2.3   Rhythmic Correction

 Below are notated various rhythmic patterns. Each contains one or more errors based on the rhythmic patterns that you will hear. Correct the errors in the notated patterns to reflect what you hear. The quarter-note pulse is given before the pattern is played.

A.

B.

C.

D.

EXERCISE 2.4   Rhythmic Pattern Drills

 Notate below the rhythmic pattern that you hear. The quarter-note pulse is given before hearing each example.

     A.

     B.

C.

D.

EXERCISE 2.5　Rhythmic Values

Subdivide each of the rhythmic series below into various rhythmic groupings, each of which sums to the original value. Follow the instructions for each exercise. You have at your disposal the following devices: shorter note values, ties, dots, rests, and alternate groupings. There are two sample solutions below.

Sample solution 1: given is a dotted quarter note, followed by various divisions:

1.

Sample solution 2: given is a measure of four quarter notes and various subdivisions:

2.

Exercises. Given:

3.

Complete the following tasks, maintaining the total duration of each of the given values:

A　Write six different rhythmic solutions, each of which contains ever-shorter note values.

B.　Write four different solutions, each of which includes the use of dotted note values.

C.　Write six different solutions, each of which includes the use of ties.

D.　Write four different solutions, each of which contains the use of rests.

EXERCISE 2.6　Meter and Mode Identification:　Simple and Compound Meters

This exercise builds on Exercise 2.3 in the text, but this time you will also hear compound meters (that is, meters in which the beat is divided into three parts). Your choices are: $\frac{2}{4}$, $\frac{3}{4}$, $\frac{4}{4}$, and $\frac{6}{8}$. There may be more than a single right answer, given that perception of meter is often based on an individual's perception. For example, one person may hear a waltz that is written in $\frac{3}{4}$ (i.e., a simple triple meter) as being in $\frac{6}{8}$ (i.e., a compound duple meter). This is because the rapid tempo groups the three beats of a measure into a single large beat, creating a measure of $\frac{3}{8}$. And, since there is often an accent on measures 1 and 3 in a four-measure unit, the listener may hear two of the $\frac{3}{4}$ measures as a single measure of $\frac{6}{8}$.

A. Brahms, "Wie Melodien zieht es mir" ("As If Melodies Were Moving"), *Five Songs for High Voice and Piano*, op. 105, no. 1: meter: _____ mode:_____

B. Chopin, Prelude in F minor, op. 28, no. 18, BI 107: meter: _____ mode:_____

C. Ward "And the Band Played On": meter: _____ mode:_____

D. Schumann, "Reiterstück," *Album für die Jugend*, op. 85, no. 21: meter: _____ mode:_____

E. Bach, Prelude in B♭ major, *Well-Tempered Clavier*, Book 1, BWV 866: meter: ____ mode:_____

EXERCISE 2.7   Adding Bar Lines

The following three sets of rhythms have a meter signature but no bar lines. Supply bar lines based on the meter signature, and, if necessary, clarify the meter. After adding the bar lines, conduct the meter, and either clap or speak the rhythms.

Sample:

EXERCISE 2.8   Determining Meter and Adding Bar Lines

The following examples are unmetered (some are familiar tunes). Sing through the tunes, trying to determine the best meter according to the following criteria:

- Long notes usually fall on an accented part of the measure. Shorter notes usually follow longer notes and fall on an unaccented part of the measure.
- Changes in melodic contour often coincide with a downbeat or accented beat.
- All examples are in major. Note that $\hat{1}$, $\hat{3}$, and $\hat{5}$ often occur on accented beats.

After you determine the meter and add bar lines, sing the tune again while conducting.

A.   Sample Solution:

B.

C.

D.

E.

EXERCISE 2.9   Matching

This exercise is identical to Exercise 2.2, but this time triplets are included. Note: There may be more than a single correct answer, and not every letter is matched with a number. The first example in column A is completed for you.

EXERCISE 2.10   Rhythmic Correction

Below are several metered examples, each of which contains numerous rhythmic errors: there are too few or too many beats within most measures. Circle, then change when necessary, one or more given rhythmic values in each measure in order to make the measure agree with the time signature. Do not change rests or eliminate or add any notes. There may be many ways to correct a measure.

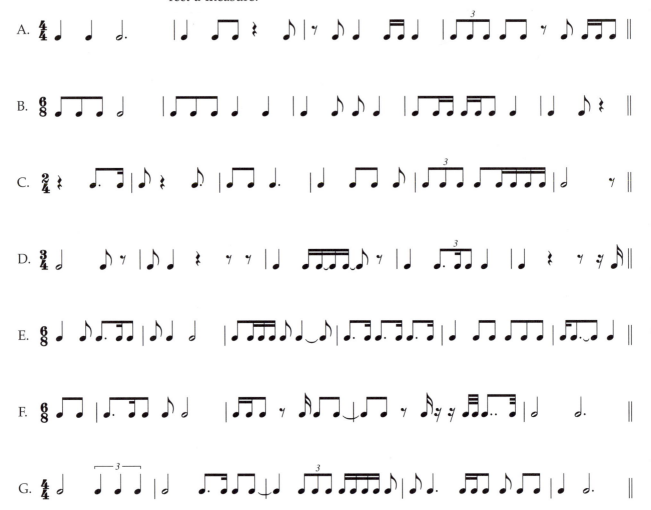

EXERCISE 2.11   Conducting and Singing Fragments in Rhythm and Meter

This exercise presents melodic fragments in a meter, with a rhythmic pattern given below. First, practice the conducting patterns for $\frac{2}{4}$, $\frac{3}{4}$, $\frac{4}{4}$, and $\frac{6}{8}$. Then, using "ta" or other rhythmic syllables, conduct the meter and say the rhythm. Finally, conduct the meter and sing the scale degrees in rhythm. Continue each pattern until you return to the tonic.

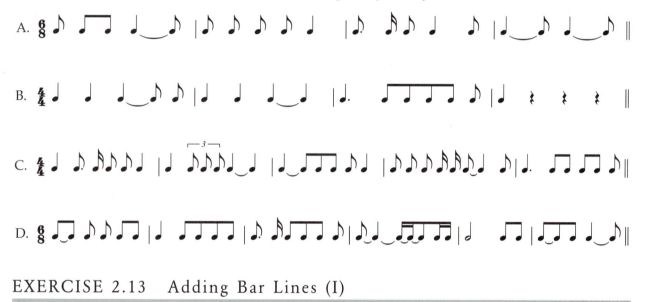

EXERCISE 2.12   Beaming

Below are examples whose rhythmic notation does not reflect the given meter clearly. Clap each rhythm. Then, clarify the meter by renotating each example with beams of appropriate length. When you have corrected the notation, conduct the meter and either clap or say the rhythms.

EXERCISE 2.13   Adding Bar Lines (I)

Renotate rhythms that extend over bars by replacing any note that does not fit in a measure with two smaller ones tied together. Then add beams. Note: Examples begin on downbeats but might not end on downbeats. If they do not, add any necessary rests. When you have added the bar lines, conduct the meter and either clap or say the rhythms.

EXERCISE 2.14   Adding Bar Lines (II)

This exercise is identical to Exercise 2.13. Keep the following in mind:

1. All examples begin on the downbeat, but they need not end on downbeats.
2. Do not change the given rhythms.
3. Maintain the prevailing "feel" of the meter; that is, do not contradict the given meter. For example, given that $^6_8$ is generally felt in two large beats, group values around those metrical accents.

When you have added the bar lines, conduct the meter and either clap or say the rhythms.

EXERCISE 2.15   Determining Meter and Adding Bar Lines (I)

Determine the best meter for each of the melodies below. Then, add a meter signature and bar lines. Remember, tunes may start with an anacrusis.

EXERCISE 2.16   Determining Meter and Adding Bar Lines (II)

Study and perform the unmetered rhythms below in order to determine a probable meter. Choose the one that places the most occurrences of a longer duration on a downbeat. Add bar lines and, when necessary, ties. Be aware that the normal groupings of note values may not be observed. For example, beams that group two eighth notes in simple and three in compound are not included. Examples may start with an anacrusis, and they need not end on downbeats. There may be more than one possible meter for some examples.

EXERCISE 2.17   Determining Meter and Adding Bar Lines (III)

Determine the meter and add bar lines for each of the following examples drawn from the literature; there may be more than one possible answer. Begin by "scanning" the rhythms, noting repetitions that create larger patterns. Recall that accent, and therefore metrical emphasis, is often enhanced by durational accents, changes of harmony, musical patterning, texture, register, and so on. List at least three criteria that you used in order to determine each example's meter.

A.   Bach, Prelude No. 2 in D minor, *Clavier-büchlein für W.Fr. Bach*, BWV 926

B.   Grieg, "Melodie" ("Melody"), *Lyriske stykke IV (Lyric Pieces IV)* op. 47. no. 3

C.   Bach, Prelude no. 4 in A minor, from Sechs kleine Préludien, BWV 942

D1.   Grieg, "Arietta," *Lyriske stykke I* (*Lyric Pieces I*), op. 12, no. 1. This is the first of Grieg's sixty-six Lyric Pieces. The second excerpt, "Remembrances," was written almost a half-century later and is the last Lyric Piece. They are obviously contrasting works, but do you notice any similarities?

D2.   Grieg, "Efterklang" ("Remembrances"), *Lyriske stykke X* (*Lyric Pieces X*), op. 71, no. 7

EXERCISE 2.18   Singing Rhythmic-Metric Disruptions

Below are melodic fragments that illustrate syncopation and hemiola. Label and bracket examples of these disruptions. Then, sing each pattern, continuing it until you return to the tonic. Finally, be able to conduct yourself while singing. Example A has been labeled for you.

EXERCISE 2.19   Analysis of Rhythmic-Metric Disruptions

Label and bracket examples of syncopation and hemiola in the examples below.

A.   Brahms, *Allegro non troppo*, Violin Concerto, op. 77

B.   Brahms, "Variation 7," *Variations on a Theme by Haydn*, op. 56b

(*Continued*)

(*Continued*)

EXERCISE 2.20   Transforming Melodic Fragments

Sing each fragment as written and in any other major or minor key. Continue the pattern until you return to the tonic. Then, transform the tunes by adding syncopations or hemiolas. The easiest way to disrupt the rhythms is to move strong-beat accents to a weak beat by making the strong-beat duration shorter than that of the weak beat.

EXERCISE 2.21   Scale Analysis from the Literature: Major Keys

Determine the initial key of the excerpt, then bracket new major-key areas as they occur. Begin by looking for accidentals, since they imply a new tonal area. This method will reduce the twelve possible keys to only one, or at the most two. For example, if you encounter two sharps, F♯ and C♯, then you know that the major scale/key is D, since D major contains two sharps (review the circle of fifths, if necessary). Then, on a separate sheet, notate the scales in ascending form and in the order that they appear.

A.   Schumann, "Ihre Stimme" ("Your Voice"), op. 96, no. 3

B.

C.   After Mozart, *Andante*, Violin Sonata in A major, K. 402

D.   After Haydn, Symphony No. 38 in C major, Hob. I. 38

EXERCISE 2.22   Scale Analysis: Minor Keys

This exercise is identical to Exercise 2.21, but now each example contains two or more minor or major scales. Follow the instructions in Exercise 2.21, but recall the added dimension of the leading tone in minor: $\hat{7}$ will need to be raised to create a leading tone, so you will encounter one more accidental in each key than is found in the key signature. For example, the key of B minor contains two sharps, F♯ and C♯, but you will also find A♯ which, of course, is not in the key signature, but is necessary in order to raise $\hat{7}$ to become a leading tone.

A.   Mozart, Symphony No. 40 in G minor, K. 550

EXERCISE 2.23   Keyboard: Scales in Rhythm

Play the major and three forms of minor scales (natural, harmonic, and melodic) in keys with three sharps and three flats. Determine a probable meter for each exercise. Use the tetrachordal fingering. Sing as you play.

EXERCISE 2.24   Keyboard: Scale Fragments in Rhythm

Sing each fragment in rhythm. Then, tap the beat (for simple meters, it will be the quarter note and for compound, the dotted quarter note) while you sing. Next, play the melodic fragments in rhythm on the piano with either hand while tapping the beat with the free hand. Finally, determine a possible meter for each example and conduct that meter while playing the melodic fragments.

EXERCISE 2.25   Keyboard: Scale Fragments in Both Hands

Using both hands, which are placed one octave apart, play the following scale degree patterns. Then, play the patterns in either hand while singing it. Finally, try playing and/or singing the first three exercises by beginning one hand before the second hand. Start the second hand as the first plays the third note of the pattern. Try singing and playing this way as well. Such **canons** are common in tonal music.

scale degrees in A minor:	$\hat{1}$	$\hat{2}$	$\hat{3}$	$\hat{2}$	$\hat{1}$			Now try in B♭ major
scale degrees in D minor:	$\hat{3}$	$\hat{2}$	$\hat{1}$	$\hat{2}$	$\hat{3}$			Now try in E♭ major
scale degrees in G minor:	$\hat{5}$	$\hat{4}$	$\hat{3}$	$\hat{2}$	$\hat{3}$	$\hat{2}$	$\hat{1}$	Now try in D major
scale degrees in A major:	$\hat{6}$	$\hat{7}$	$\hat{8}$	$\hat{3}$	$\hat{1}$			Now try in F♯ minor
scale degrees in F major and C minor:	$\hat{4}$	$\hat{5}$	$\hat{6}$	$\hat{5}$	$\hat{2}$			

EXERCISE 2.26   Keyboard: Two-Notes in the Right Hand

Using only your right hand, simultaneously play the following pairs of scale degrees. As you play, sing both pitches, first the lower then the higher. Choose a comfortable singing range somewhere around middle C.

A. Play $\hat{1}$ and $\hat{5}$ (using fingers 1 and 5) for the following keys:

      G major
      B♭ major
      E major

In left hand: D minor
      B minor
      F minor

B. Play $\hat{1}$ and $\hat{3}$ (using fingers 1 and 3) for the following keys:

      C major
      B♭ major
      D major

In left hand: A minor
      E minor
      G minor

C. Play $\hat{2}$ and $\hat{5}$ (using fingers 2 and 5) for the following keys:

      A major
      B major
      G major

In left hand: C minor
      D minor
      B minor

D. Play $\hat{1}$ and $\hat{4}$ (using fingers 1 and 4) for the following keys:

      A major
      B major
      G major

In left hand: C minor
      D minor
      B minor

E. Play $\hat{2}$ and $\hat{4}$ (using fingers 2 and 4) for the following keys:

      B♭ major
      F major
      A major

In left hand: B minor
      C♯ minor
      A minor

EXERCISE 2.27   Keyboard: Singing Pitches

Return to Exercise 2.26. For Examples A–E, sing one of the pitches at the same time you play the other. Begin by playing the lower pitch, then sing the upper pitch. After you feel comfortable with this, play the upper pitch and sing the lower pitch. Be sure to find a comfortable singing range.

CHAPTER 3

Intervals and Melody

EXERCISE 3.1   Identification of Perfect, Major, and Minor Intervals

Identify only the perfect, major, and minor intervals; label the remaining dissonant intervals "D." Use the analytical technique that views the lower note as the tonic of a scale.

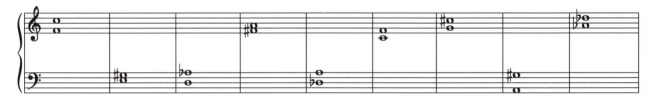

EXERCISE 3.2   Writing Intervals

Complete the following tasks, making sure that you maintain the generic (numerical) size. For example, increasing the size of a P4 by a half step creates an A4, not a d5.

A. What would the following intervals become if you increase their size by a semitone?

P5
m3
M2
M7
d3
d8

B. What would the following intervals become if you decrease their size by a semitone?

m6
M3
P4
A6
A8

C.   Name the pitches that occur above A, C, and E♭ at the:

	A	C	E♭
P4			
m3			
M7			
d8			
m2			
A5			

Name the pitches that occur below D, B♭, and F at the:

	D	B♭	F
M2			
P5			
m3			
D5			
M7			

D.   Notate the following intervals above the given pitches:

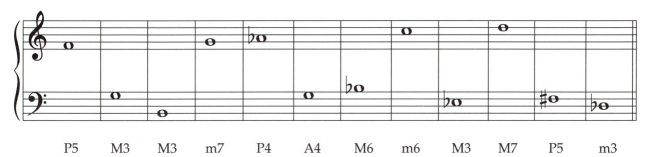

P5   M3   M3   m7   P4   A4   M6   m6   M3   M7   P5   m3

E.   Notate the following intervals below the given pitches:

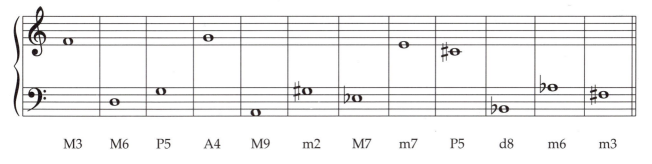

M3   M6   P5   A4   M9   m2   M7   m7   P5   d8   m6   m3

EXERCISE 3.3   Notating Intervals

Notate the intervals in the required clefs:

A. treble clef: major seconds above and below:

   F
   A
   C
   B♭
   F♯

B.   treble clef: minor thirds above and below:

   G
   B

    E♭
    G♭
    A♭

C. bass clef: perfect fourths above and below:

    F
    A♭
    D
    E
    B

D. alto clef: minor sixths above and below:

    E♭
    B♭
    C♯

E. treble clef: augmented seconds above and below:

    C
    A♭
    G

F. bass clef: minor sevenths above and below:

    D
    F
    A

EXERCISE 3.4   Identifying Intervals

Identify each interval below.

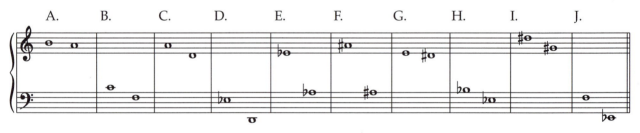

EXERCISE 3.5   Identifying and Notating Seconds, Perfect Fifths, and Octaves (I)

Complete and identify the interval. The second note is given. Your choices are: m2, M2, P5, P8, or compounds.

EXERCISE 3.6 Identifying and Notating Seconds, Perfect Fifths, and Octaves (II)

 You now hear descending seconds, fifths, and octaves. For Examples A–E, the first note is given and for F–J, the second. Compound intervals are included in this exercise. Label all intervals.

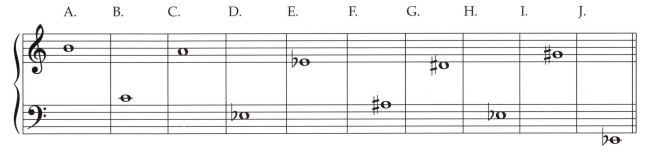

EXERCISE 3.7 Identifying and Notating Seconds and All Perfect Intervals

 A mix of ascending and descending seconds, fourths, fifths, and octaves occurs. Notate and label intervals. For Examples A–E, the first note is given and for F–J, the second.

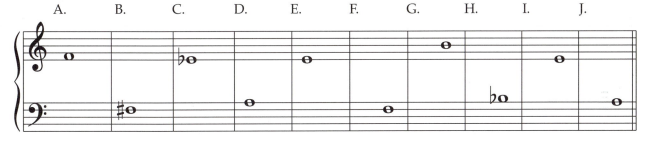

EXERCISE 3.8 Identifying and Notating Seconds and Perfect Intervals

 You will hear intervals played harmonically (simultaneously). Notate and label intervals. For Examples A–E, the lower note is given, and for F–J, the upper.

EXERCISE 3.9   Identifying and Notating Major and Minor Thirds and the Tritone

The lower note for melodic ascending intervals is given. Notate the second pitch and label the interval. Since the diminished fifth and augmented fourth are impossible to distinguish aurally, notate them both. Refer to compound thirds as major or minor tenths.

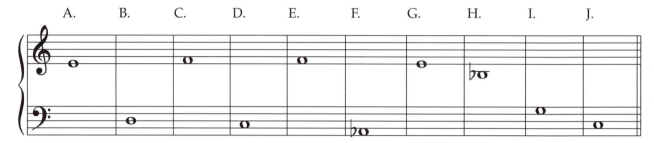

EXERCISE 3.10   Identifying and Notating Thirds and Tritones (I)

This exercise is identical to the previous except that the second, rather than the first, note is given.

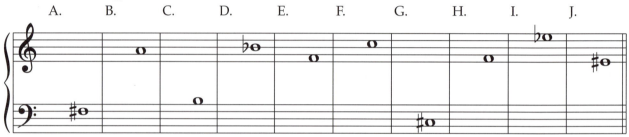

EXERCISE 3.11   Identifying and Notating Thirds and Tritones (II)

This exercise is similar to the preceding exercise, but now descending thirds and tritones occur. For Examples A–E, the first note is given and for F–J, the second.

EXERCISE 3.12   Identifying and Notating Thirds and Tritones (III)

Ascending and descending thirds and tritones occur. For Examples A–E, the first note is given and for F–J, the second.

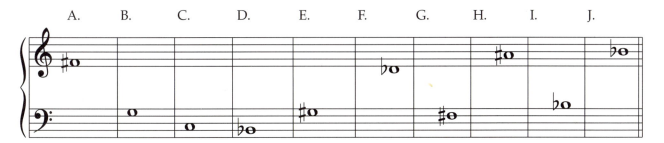

EXERCISE 3.13 Identifying and Notating Thirds and Tritones (IV)

 Thirds and tritones are played harmonically. For Examples A–E, the lower note is given, and for F–J, the upper.

EXERCISE 3.14 Intervals: Seconds, Thirds, Fourths, Fifths, Octaves, and Tritones (I)

 Notate and label the ascending or descending intervals that you hear. The first note is given in A–E, the second in F–J.

EXERCISE 3.15 Intervals: Seconds, Thirds, Fourths, Fifths, Octaves, and Tritones (II)

Notate and label the harmonic intervals that you hear. The lower note is given in A–E, the upper in F–J.

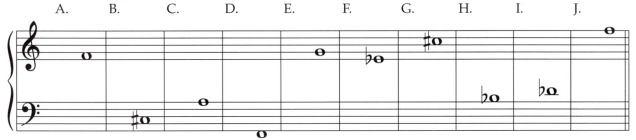

EXERCISE 3.16   Notation of Diatonic Melodies

You will hear six short melodic fragments (around eight notes). Once you are given the tonality, quietly sing $\hat{1}$–$\hat{3}$–$\hat{5}$–$\hat{3}$–$\hat{1}$ in order to give you a tonal footing, then memorize each fragment. Finally, notate the fragment using scale degree numbers.

A.

B.

C.

D.

E.

F.

EXERCISE 3.17   Notation of Melodic Fragments

This exercise is identical to the previous one, except that this time you are to notate the pitches on staff paper (noteheads without stems are adequate, since rhythm is not involved at this point) in the following keys:

A.   E minor
B.   F major
C.   F♯ minor
D.   C major
E.   G minor
F.   D major

Include an analysis of scale degrees and the intervals between each pair of pitches.

EXERCISE 3.18   Intervals: M6 and m6 and 7ths; Review of Seconds, Thirds, Fourths, Fifths, and Tritones

You will hear ascending melodic forms of the m2, M2, m3, M3, m6, M6, and m7, M7, P4, P5, and tritone. The first note is given; notate the second and label the interval.

EXERCISE 3.19 M6, m6, M7, m7; Review of Seconds, Thirds, Fourths, Fifths, and Tritones

 This exercise is identical to the previous one except that the second pitch descends.

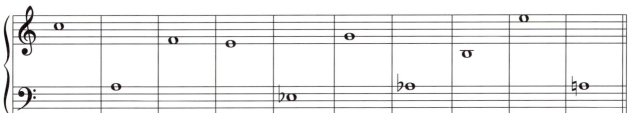

EXERCISE 3.20 Major and Minor Sixths and Sevenths; Review of Seconds, Thirds, Fourths, Fifths, and Tritones

This exercise is similar to Exercise 3.19, but now intervals are presented harmonically. Identify each on a separate sheet of paper.

EXERCISE 3.21 Identifying All Intervals

You will hear a mix of melodic, harmonic, and ascending and descending intervals. Identify each on a separate sheet of paper.

EXERCISE 3.22 Keyboard: Scales

Play major and minor scales with key signatures up to and including four sharps and four flats. Use the tetrachord fingering introduced in Chapter 1.

EXERCISE 3.23 Keyboard: Scales and Intervals

Using one finger in each hand, play the following scale degree pairs in the following keys: A♭, A, E♭, and E major and F, F♯, C, and C♯ minor. Be able to identify the melodic interval. Scale degrees:

$\hat{1} + \hat{4}$
$\hat{1} + \hat{6}$
$\hat{2} + \hat{4}$
$\hat{2} + \hat{6}$
$\hat{4} + \hat{7}$
$\hat{5} + \hat{3}$

EXERCISE 3.24 Keyboard: Two-Voice Step Motions in Parallel Motion

Play the two-voice exercises that focus on steps (that is, the interval of the second). Play each exercise in major and minor keys up to and including four sharps and four flats in a steady tempo. The lowest note in each exercise, $\hat{1}$, should be played using the thumb in the right hand and the fifth finger in the left hand.

Play adjacent notes with adjacent fingers. Be able to sing one part while playing the other.

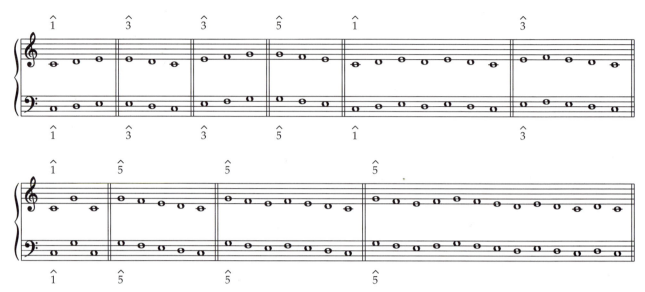

EXERCISE 3.25   Keyboard: Seconds, Fifths, and Fourths

Using the instructions from the previous exercise, play the exercises below.

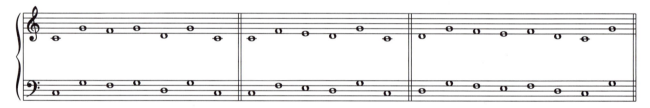

EXERCISE 3.26   Keyboard: More Interval Play

Below is a series of notated pitches. Sing the given pitch, then say the letter name and play major and minor thirds, tritones, and perfect fifths and fourths above and below the given pitches.

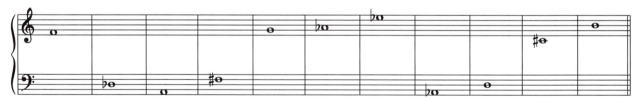

EXERCISE 3.27   Keyboard: Still More Interval Play

Given the series of pitches below, find a comfortable register in which you can sing the required intervals above and below the given pitch.

1. Given: E. Play and sing major and minor thirds and perfect fifths.
2. Given: A♭. Play and sing major and minor thirds, tritones, and perfect fifths.
3. Given: B. Play and sing all major and minor seconds and thirds and perfect intervals.

    4.   Given: E♭. Play and sing all perfect intervals and major and minor seconds
        and thirds.

EXERCISE 3.28   Keyboard: Two-Voice Exercises in Parallel Motion: Seconds and Thirds

Play the short melodies below; duplicate at the octave in the left hand. Follow the instructions for Exercise 3.24, transposing to G and E major and minor. Finally, play the left hand a sixth or tenth below what is written in the right hand, using the diatonic pitches from the key you are in. The result will be parallel sixth and parallel tenth motion. Reverse this process so that the right hand plays tenths and sixths above the left hand's given pitches.

EXERCISE 3.29   Keyboard: Interval Play at the Keyboard

Sing the given pitches below, say the letter name, then play major and minor thirds, sixths, and sevenths above and below the given pitches. Finally, be able to sing the pitch and the interval above and below before you play it.

EXERCISE 3.30   Keyboard: More Interval Play

Play each pitch below in any register, then play the required intervals above and below that pitch. Finally, find a comfortable register in which you can sing the required intervals above and below the given pitch.

1.   Given: F. Play major and minor sixths and thirds.
2.   Given: D. Play major and minor sevenths and sixths.
3.   Given: F♯. Play major and minor sevenths and thirds and perfect fifths.
4.   Given: B. Play major and minor thirds, sixths, and sevenths.
5.   Given: A. Play any of the intervals.
6.   Given: E♭. Play and sing all perfect intervals and major and minor seconds and sixths.

EXERCISE 3.31   Melodies: Temporal Elements Added

You will hear five short melodies. Determine the following:

1. meter
2. number of measures
3. prevailing rhythmic motive (notate rhythm)

Be able to sing back the entire melody. Optional: Notate in a key of your choice.

EXERCISE 3.32   Scale Analysis: Major and Minor Keys

Two or more major and/or minor keys occur in each of the following examples. Use accidentals as clues: changes in type and number of accidentals signal a change in key. For example, a shift from flats to sharps or vice versa is a clear indication that the key has changed. Similarly, an addition or reduction in the number of accidentals indicates a new key. Bracket and label each key area. Then, notate the scales that appear in each example.

A.

B.

C. Modeled on Haydn, *Fantasia*, String Quartet in E♭ major, op. 76, no. 6, Hob. III. 80

EXERCISE 3.33   Melodies from the Literature

On a separate sheet of paper, determine meter and number of measures for the following five melodies. Also, using scale degrees, label first and last note and lowest and highest.

EXERCISE 3.34   Writing Melodies

Write two or three short (twelve to sixteen pitches) unmetered melodies in major and minor keys. Strive for the characteristics of a good melody given in the text.

CHAPTER 4

Controlling Dissonance and Consonance:
Two-Voice Counterpoint

EXERCISE 4.1   Two-Part Writing (I): Error Detection

Below are three first-species two-voice counterpoints that contain two types of errors: dissonant intervals (2, 4, 7) and parallel perfect intervals (U, 5, and 8). You will label each interval, circle the errors, and specify the type of error ("D" for dissonance and "PPI" for parallel perfect intervals). Then rewrite each of the counterpoint lines using only consonant intervals (do not change the cantus). Remember, (1) aim for contrary motion, and (2) when writing in parallel motion, use only imperfect intervals. Try to make each line as stepwise (singable) as possible, and restrict non-stepwise motions mostly to skips of a third, with only one larger leap of a fourth or fifth. Avoid larger leaps altogether.

A.   counterpoint

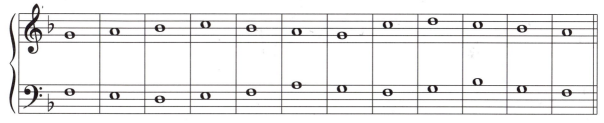

cantus

Key:

counterpoint

cantus

Key:

(Continued)

(Continued)

B. counterpoint

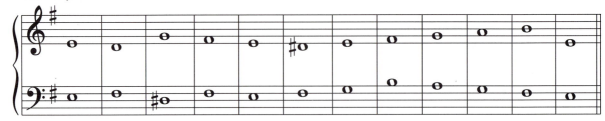

cantus

Key:

counterpoint

cantus

Key:

C. cantus

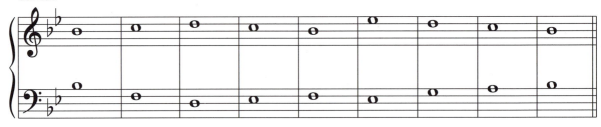

counterpoint

Key:

cantus

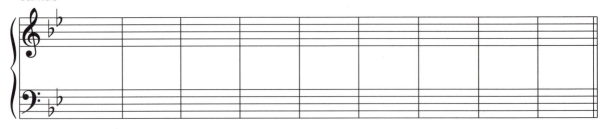

counterpoint

Key:

EXERCISE 4.2 Two-Part Writing (First Species)

Below are several cantus firmi. Write first-species (that is, note-against-note) counterpoint such that by itself it is a good melody, with a pleasing melodic arch, mostly stepwise, and easy to sing. There may be a few leaps in the counterpoint voice, but remember that thirds are most common, and leaps by fourth or fifth may occur no more than once in each exercise. Label each vertical interval (between your counterpoint and the cantus firmus), making sure that there are no dissonances and that any parallel intervals are restricted to thirds and sixths. Do not change any of the pitches of the cantus firmus.

Once you have completed writing your counterpoint, try inverting the parts; that is, if you wrote counterpoint above a cantus, place it an octave (or two) below, and vice versa. Does your solution still work (i.e., how are the melodic shapes and vertical intervals between the cantus and the counterpoint)? If it doesn't work, why not?

A.

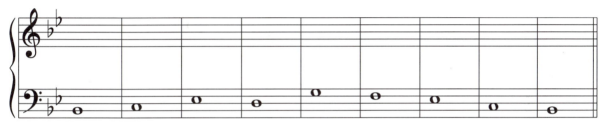

B.

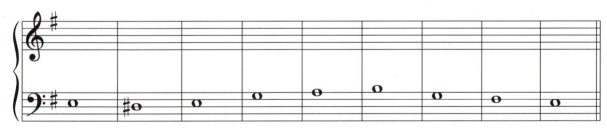

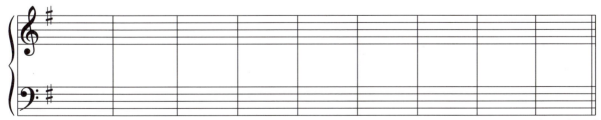

(Continued)

(Continued)

C.

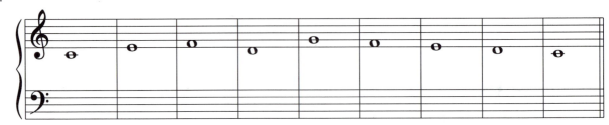

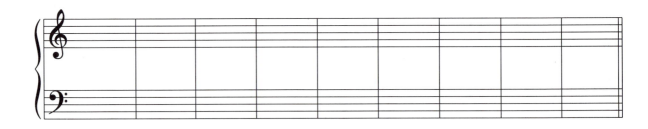

D.

EXERCISE 4.3   Analysis of Contrapuntal Motions

Determine the predominant contrapuntal motion in each of the two-voice examples below. Then, using brackets, label two or more instances where other types of contrapuntal motions occur. Your choices are: parallel (p), similar (s), oblique (o), or contrary (c).

A.   Bach, Duette no. 1 in E minor, BWV 802

B.   Bach, Duette no. 4 in A minor, BWV 805

C.   **Andante doloroso**

D.

Canto

La pia - ga c'ho nel co - re Don - na

Basso

La pia - ga c'ho nel co - re Don - na

E.   **Allegretto**

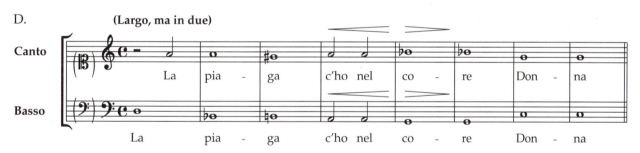

A - man - ti co - stan - ti se - gua - ci d'o -
Oh, come, faith - ful lov - ers, in hap - py ac -

F.   **Allegretto alla zingarese**

EXERCISE 4.4   Two-Part Writing (Second Species): Error Detection

We now analyze and write second-species counterpoint. Label each interval and circle and label each error according to the model analysis in A. Then rewrite each example, correcting the errors.

A.   Model analyses:

1.   (error free)
2.   (error ridden)

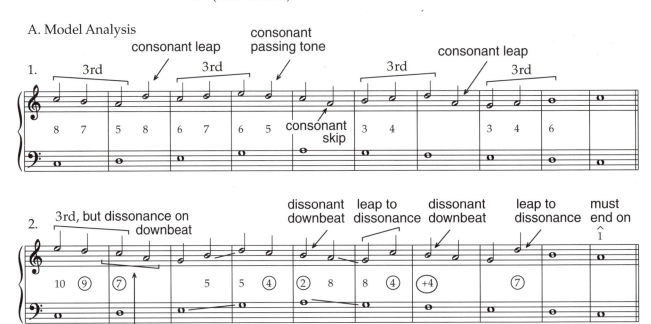

B.

C.

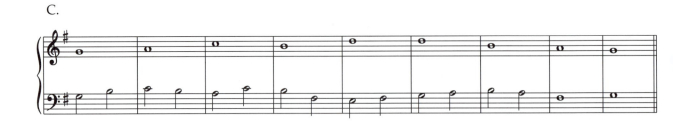

EXERCISE 4.5   Two-Part Writing (Second Species and Consonance)

We now write second-species counterpoint (two half notes in the counterpoint for each whole note in the cantus). For this exercise, use only consonance; thus you may use steps (but only those involving the interval of a fifth to a sixth or vice versa), consonant skips, or consonant leaps. Label all resulting intervals.

A.

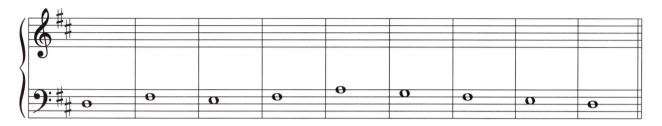

B.

EXERCISE 4.6   Two-Part Writing (Second Species: Dissonance and Consonance)

In this exercise you may use leaps (to consonances) and passing dissonance. Remember, however, that all dissonance:

1. must occur only on a weak beat.
2. must pass by filling the interval of a third.

A.

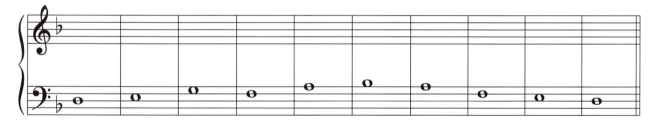

B.

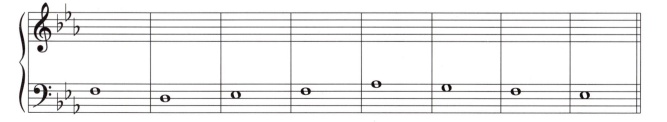

C.

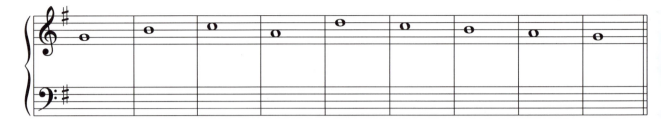

EXERCISE 4.7　Dictation: Notation of One Voice in Two-Voice Counterpoint (I)

 Following are a number of examples of two-voice counterpoint, but only the cantus firmus is given. Using your ear and knowledge of allowable pitches, notate the counterpointing voice. Check your work by labeling each interval, making sure each is consonant.

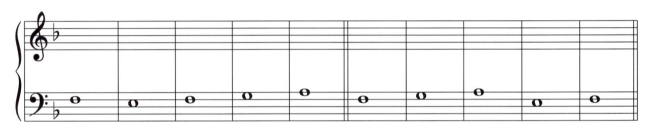

EXERCISE 4.8　Dictation: Notation of One Voice in Two-Voice Counterpoint (II)

 This exercise is identical to Exercise 4.7, except that this time the counterpoint will be notated below the cantus. Follow guidelines given in Exercise 4.7.

EXERCISE 4.9　Dictation: Notation of One Voice in Two-Voice Counterpoint (III)

 This time you will hear a counterpoint that moves in second species (that is, twice as fast as the cantus). Notate the counterpoint above the cantus and label each interval.

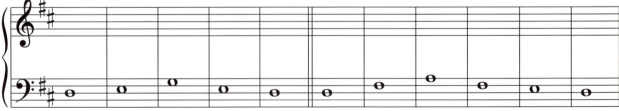

EXERCISE 4.10 Dictation: Notation of One Voice in Two-Voice Counterpoint (IV)

Notate the second species counterpoint below the cantus and label each interval.

EXERCISE 4.11 Analysis/Error Detection

Listen to the examples below that mix 1:1 and 2:1 counterpoint. Determine if what you hear is what is notated. If it is, write yes, but if not, cross out the incorrect pitch(es) and write in the correct letter name. There may be up to four errors within an exercise. Label each example's key beneath the bass clef.

EXERCISE 4.12 Notation of Two-Voice Counterpoint

You will hear short examples of two-voice counterpoint that move primarily in note-against-note style, but this time, there is an important change: you will need to notate both the upper and the lower voice using the rhythms provided. A few pitches are provided. Check your work by analyzing each interval: all verticalities must be consonant (6, 3, 5, or 8), and weak-beat moving lines (oblique motion) may be dissonant (2, 4, and 7) but the dissonance must pass.

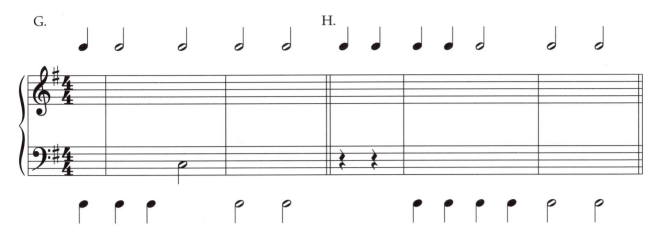

G. H.

EXERCISE 4.13 Dictation: More Notation of Two-Voice Counterpoint

Notate the following two-voice exercises. Analyze your work by labeling each interval, making sure you have notated only consonant intervals, save for the tritone. In this exercise, there are no rhythmic hints given, though a few pitches are provided. Examples A, B, and C are in B♭ major and D and E are in G minor.

A. B.

C. D.

E.

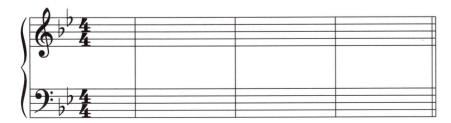

EXERCISE 4.14   Analysis

The two examples below contain a mixture of parallel, contrary, similar, and oblique motions. Listen to the minuet.

1. Label each interval in measures 1–4.
2. Study the entire excerpt for any extended passages of three or more beats that contain exclusively parallel, contrary, or oblique motions. Bracket and label these passages.
3. Are there any passages of one or two measures that contain repeated material? Is the repeated material in the same or in different voices? Is it literal or modified? Explain, citing specific measure numbers.
4. In what key does the excerpt begin? What key does it end in?
5. Is there a climax? If so, where is it and how does Telemann create it?

A.   Telemann, Minuet in C minor, *50 Minuets for Keyboard*

B.   Clementi, Sonata in G major, op. 40, no. 1

1. There is an important relationship between the two voices of this piece. In order to determine what it is, begin by scanning the lines, noting their contours. Compare the lines by writing down the generic interval size and direction for the first six notes of the right and left hands.
2. In what key does the excerpt begin? Does it end in this key? If not, where does it close?
3. Where is the most dissonant area in the excerpt? Label the intervals in this passage.
4. Is there a climax in the excerpt? If so, where? List two or three musical features that contribute to the climactic effect.

EXERCISE 4.15 Keyboard: Two-Voice Exercises

Below are exercises that contain various contrapuntal motions. All are written within the interval of a fifth: the lowest notes will be played by fifth and first fingers in left and right hands, respectively. Play as written and in the minor mode with a steady tempo. Begin by playing each hand separately; add the second hand only when you are comfortable with each hand alone. Transpose each to the keys of G, E, and B♭ major and minor. Be able to sing one part while playing the other. Finally, analyze each exercise, marking the intervals and the types of contrapuntal motions.

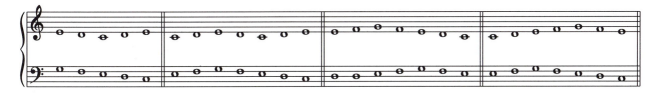

CHAPTER 5

Triads, Inversions, Figured Bass, and Harmonic Analysis

EXERCISE 5.1   Error Detection

Below are some incorrectly spelled root-position major, minor, and diminished triads. The errors include enharmonic spelling (for example, a C major triad must be spelled in thirds: C–E–G, not C–F♭–G) and wrong-note spelling (for example, a G minor triad is spelled G–B♭–D, not G–B♭–E♭). There may be no errors or as many as two, and in many cases there will be more than one correct answer. Assume that the root is correct. Correct any errors and label the triad type.

A. D–G♭–A:

B. C–D♯–G:

C. F–A♭–C♭:

D. A–C–D♯:

E. D–F–G♯:

F. B–D–F:

G. A♭–B–E♭

H. E–G–C♭:

I. C♯–E♯–G♯:

J. B♭–C♯–E♯

K. G–C♭–C×

L. D♯–E×–C♭♭

EXERCISE 5.2   Writing Root Position Triads in Close
and Open Position

Below are notated the roots of various major, minor, and diminished triads. Listen to each example, label the triad type, and then notate in close position the missing pitches of the triad. Finally, arrange each triad in an open position. There are many arrangements possible.

F major		d minor		f♯ minor		B♭ major		g diminished		A♭ major	
close	open	close	open	close	open	close	open	close	open	close	open

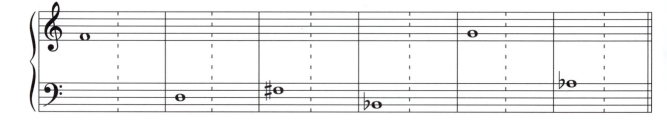

EXERCISE 5.3   Constructing Triads

 Below is a series of pitches, each of which is either the root, third, or fifth of a major, minor, or diminished triad. You will hear the given pitch, followed by the triad of which it is part. Determine the type of triad and whether the given pitch is the triad's root, third, or fifth. Then, notate the triad. There are many arrangements possible.

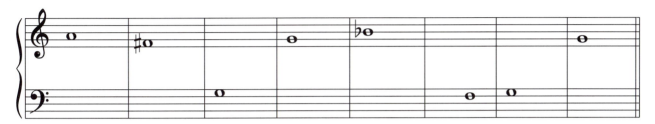

EXERCISE 5.4   Chord Quality Identification and Notation

 Each of the following pitches is the root of a triad. Write close-position triads above each given pitch. Next to these, write a version in open position.

close   open   close   open   close   open   close   open

close   open   close   open   close   open   close   open

EXERCISE 5.5   Writing Triads in Inversion and Performing Other Triadic Manipulations

A. Given the bass, notate the following in close position:

1. first-inversion major triads: D, E♭, F♯, A, B;
    second-inversion major triads: C, E, F, A♭, B♭
2. first-inversion minor triads: C♯, F, G, A♭;
    second-inversion minor triads: E♭, F♯, A, B
3. first-inversion diminished triads: B, F, C, A♭

B.   Below are various pitches; each is a potential member of nine triads (we will consider major, minor, and diminished triads only). For example, given the pitch D, it could be the following:

1.   root of a D major, D minor, or D diminished triad
2.   third of a B♭ major, B minor, or B diminished triad
3.   fifth of a G major triad or G minor triad, or G♯ diminished triad

Determine the nine potential major, minor, and diminished chords of which each of the following pitches could be members:

	root:	third:	fifth:
1. C:			
2. F:			
3. B♭:			
4. C♯:			
5. F♯:			

C.   Below are various two-note pairs. Make as many different types of triads from each pair as possible. We will consider all four triad types: major, minor, diminished, and augmented. For example, given the pair of pitches G and B, you can make four different triads: G–B–D (major), G–B–D♯ (augmented), E–G–B (minor), and E♭–G–B (augmented).

1.   A and C
2.   D and F♯
3.   B♭ and D♭
4.   F and C
5.   C and A♭
6.   C♯ and E

EXERCISE 5.6   Triad Identification: Aural Recognition

This exercise is similar to the previous exercises, but now you must rely on your ear, since the triads are not notated. Label bass member (B) as 1, 3, 5, and chord quality (Q) as M, m, d.

A. ____	____		F. ____	____
B	Q		B	Q
B. ____	____		G. ____	____
B	Q		B	Q
C. ____	____		H. ____	____
B	Q		B	Q
D. ____	____		I. ____	____
B	Q		B	Q
E. ____	____		J. ____	____
B	Q		B	Q

EXERCISE 5.7   Triad Identification: Aural Recognition

This exercise is identical to Exercise 5.6, but now you must also identify the member of the chord that is in the soprano (S) in addition to bass (B) and quality (Q).

A. ___	___	___		B. ___	___	___
B	S	Q		B	S	Q

C. __	__	__		G. __	__	__
B	S	Q		B	S	Q

D. __	__	__		H. __	__	__
B	S	Q		B	S	Q

E. __	__	__		I. __	__	__
B	S	Q		B	S	Q

F. __	__	__		J. __	__	__
B	S	Q		B	S	Q

EXERCISE 5.8 Triad Completion

Notated below are incomplete triads: only two of the three voices are provided. Listen to each example, which is played twice: the first time you will hear only the two voices; the second time you will hear the complete three-voice triad. Notate the missing member of the triad in the required register (bass = B; alto = A; soprano = S). The three types of triads (major, minor, and diminished) may be inverted. Analyze each of the triads by identifying triad type (M, m, d) and figured bass (show any chromaticism). The first example is worked for you.

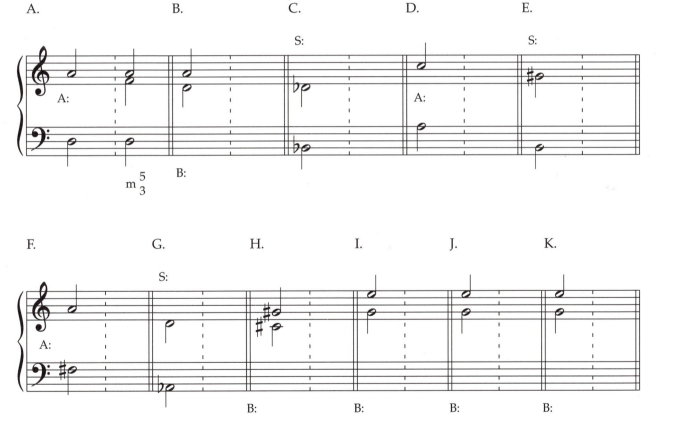

EXERCISE 5.9 Figured Bass Practice: Construction, Playing, and Singing

Construct chords above each bass note following the figured bass. There is no underlying key in this exercise, thus no key signature, so add any necessary accidentals. Provide root and quality for each. Note there is more than one pos-

sible solution. After playing the series of chords, return to the beginning of
the exercise and play only the given bass pitch, singing the intervals above as
required.

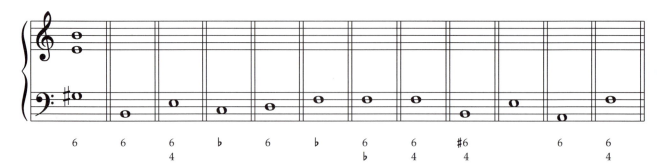

6	6	6	♭	6	♭	6	6	#6		6	6
		4					4	4			4
					♭						

EXERCISE 5.10 Analysis: Triads in Four Voices and in Various Spacings

A. Determine the root and quality of the triad.

B. Determine which member of the chord is in the bass (root [1], third [3], or
fifth [5]).

C. Determine which member of the triad is doubled (root [1], third [3], or fifth [5]).

D. Provide a full (that is, no shorthand) figured bass analysis that shows accidentals (that is, consider the exercise to be in C major).

I.

	A.	B.	C.	D.	E.	F.	G.	H.	I.	J.	K.	L.
root	A♭											
chord quality:	M											
chord member in bass	1											
doubled note:	1											
figured bass:	♭5 3											

II.

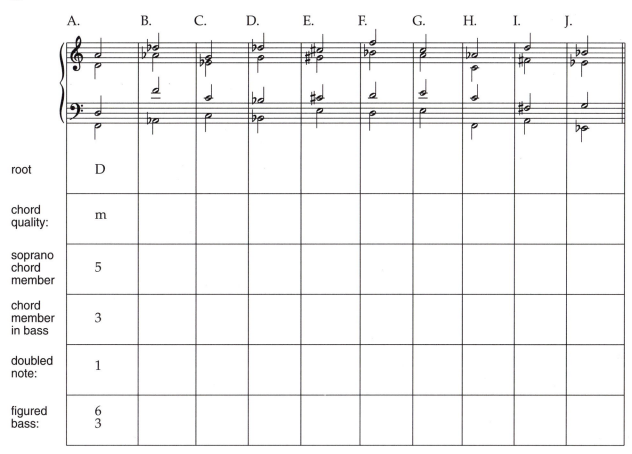

	A.	B.	C.	D.	E.	F.	G.	H.	I.	J.
root	D									
chord quality:	m									
soprano chord member	5									
chord member in bass	3									
doubled note:	1									
figured bass:	6 3									

EXERCISE 5.11   Writing Triads Generated from Various Scale Degrees

The bass notes below represent the roots of triads. The keys are given, but not their signatures. Add the third and fifth above each root in close position and determine the quality of these triads based on their scale degree. For example, consider the key of A major and the pitch C♯. Since C♯ is the root, then you are to build a triad on the mediant (iii). Since iii is a minor triad in a major key, then you must add the correct accidentals: C♯–E–G♯. Do not contradict the implied key signature; for example, there are C♯s and G♯s in the key of A major. Finally, analyze with roman numerals (RNs).

A. Given the key of D major and the following scale degrees:

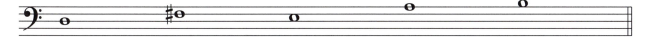

B. Given the key of B♭ major and the following scale degrees:

C. Given the key of G minor and the following scale degrees:

D. Given the key of C minor and the following scale degrees:

D. Given the key of B minor and the following scale degrees:

EXERCISE 5.12   Singing

Sing the following scale degree patterns which form triads. Determine the roman numeral of each triad.

$\hat{1}$–$\hat{3}$–$\hat{5}$ $\hat{3}$–$\hat{5}$–$\hat{8}$ $\hat{7}$–$\hat{5}$–$\hat{2}$ $\hat{1}$–$\hat{5}$–$\hat{1}$

EXERCISE 5.13   Varied Tasks

Complete the tasks below.
   Name three major and three minor keys in which each of the following triads appear. Use roman numerals for your phrases. For example: A major: V in D major, I in A major; IV in E major; iii in F♯ minor

1.   D major: _____ _____ _____ _____
2.   A minor: _____ _____ _____ _____
3.   F major: _____ _____ _____ _____
4.   B♭ major: _____ _____ _____ _____

EXERCISE 5.14   Keyboard: Triads in Various Spacings: Three Voices

Below are two pitches of a root-position triad. Determine the missing chordal member and play it below the soprano voice to create a three-part texture. If a perfect fifth is given, the triad could be major or minor; if a minor 3rd is given, the triad could be minor or diminished. Be able to play both triad types. Transpose each triad up and down a major third and a perfect fifth. Finally, be able to sing the missing note before playing it.

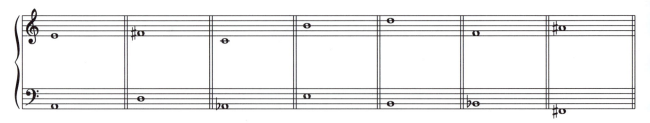

EXERCISE 5.15   Keyboard: Building Triads

The following intervals require a third note to make a triad. The lowest note is the bass, from which you will construct major, minor, and diminished triads. For example, given a perfect fifth, only a root-position triad possible; given that there are no fifths in inverted triads. Similarly, the fourth would belong only to a second inversion triad ($^6_4$). However, if a third or sixth is given, there is more than one type of triad to which they may belong. For example, the third belongs both to a root position triad ($^5_3$) and to a first-inversion triad ($^6_3$) because there is a third above the bass in both triads. Further, depending on the type of third, fifth or sixth given, three or even four triads are possible. For example, given C and E♭, you could construct C minor, C diminished, A♭ major (in $^6_3$ position) and A diminished (in $^6_3$ position) triads. Determine the missing pitch, say the triad and its position, and then play it. Where there are two or more possibilities, play them all (see examples below). Finally, spread out each triad, playing the bass in the left hand and the upper voices with the right.

exercises:

EXERCISE 5.16   Keyboard: Triads in Various Spacings: Three Voices

This exercise is similar to Exercise 5.15, except that now you will add the missing pitch either above or below the given right-hand note. First, create root-position major, minor, and diminished triads. Each example presents the opportunity to make at least two different quality triads. Then, depending on the given interval, create as many different $^6_3$ and $^6_4$ major, minor, and diminished triads as possible.

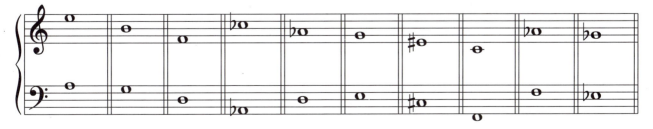

EXERCISE 5.17 Keyboard: Triads in Various Spacings: Figured Bass in Three Voices

Realize the figured bass by adding the two missing notes in the right hand. Play each harmony in two different spacings.

EXERCISE 5.18 Keyboard: Outer Voices and Keyboard Style (I)

You are given a right-hand note and its chordal function; the root of the triad appears in the bass. Complete each triad by adding the missing note. Then, add a doubled root in your right hand as close to the other two notes as possible to create a four-voice texture. Finally, arpeggiate the right hand chord while sustaining the left-hand note. An example is given below.

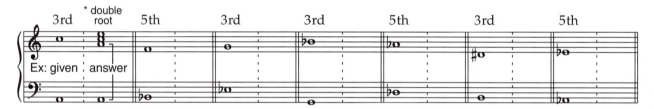

EXERCISE 5.19 Keyboard: Outer Voices and Keyboard Style (II)

A soprano and bass appear below. The bass is always the root of the triad. Determine the chordal function of the soprano, then add the missing triad note(s) below the soprano; double the root. Play three voices in the right hand and the root in the left. Analyze with roman numerals.

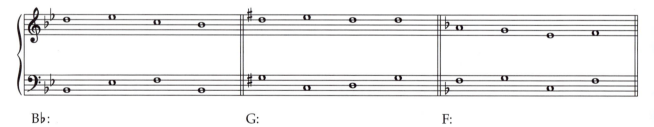

EXERCISE 5.20 Keyboard: Soprano Voice and Building Chords (I)

You are given a soprano line, the chordal function of each note (1 = root, 3 = third, 5 = fifth), and the key. Play the resulting triads below the soprano using keyboard style (three pitches in the right hand and one in the left hand) to create a four-voice texture. The root will be in the bass. Name the quality of each triad. Note: triads built on $\hat{5}$ will be major in both major and minor keys; that is, raise $\hat{7}$.

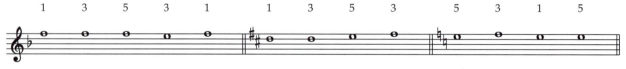

EXERCISE 5.21   Keyboard: Soprano Voice and Building Chords (II)

This exercise is similar to the preceding exercise. Now, however, you are given the soprano and the letter name of the triad. Add necessary pitches below the soprano to create complete right-hand triads; then double the root in the bass to create a four-voice keyboard-style texture.

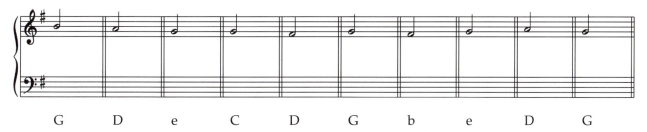

G   D   e   C   D   G   b   e   D   G

EXERCISE 5.22   Keyboard: More Triads and Doublings

Inversions are included in this exercise. Add missing pitches in the right hand below the soprano to create full triads, and play the bass note as required by the figured bass in the left hand. Remember to double the root of the chord.

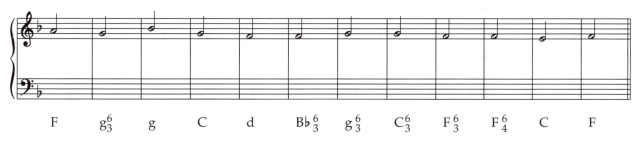

F   g⁶₃   g   C   d   B♭⁶₃   g⁶₃   C⁶₃   F⁶₃   F⁶₄   C   F

EXERCISE 5.23   Keyboard: Figured Bass and Doublings

In keyboard style, realize the two figured basses below. Double the root in each example. Move the right hand the shortest possible distance, by step preferably, when shifting to the next chord.

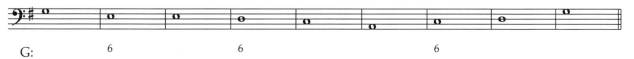

G: 6   6   6

d: 6   6   ♭   6   ♯

EXERCISE 5.24   Analysis

The following four-voice chord progressions contain triads in root position and in various inversions.

 1.   Label the key.

2. Identify triad roots with roman numerals.
3. Include a figured bass for inverted triads.

KEY:

KEY:

EXERCISE 5.25   Analysis

Label the key for each example below. Provide roman numerals and figured bass for each harmony. In the spaces above each chord, provide both the scale degree number and chordal member of the doubled pitches within the chord.

scale degree of doubled pitch:

chordal member of doubled pitch:

scale degree of doubled pitch:

chordal member of doubled pitch:

CHAPTER 6

Seventh Chords, Texture, and Musical Hierarchy

EXERCISE 6.1 Aural and Visual Analysis: Identification of Root-Position Seventh Chords

 Listen to the following series of root-position seventh chords that are written in close position. Identify the type of seventh chord by choosing among Mm (major-minor), MM (major), mm (minor), dm (half diminished, ⌀7), and dd (diminished, °7). Then, transform each seventh chord type as follows: Mm⟷dd, MM⟷dm, mm⟷Mm. Notate the transformed chord in the space provided, but in the opposite clef in which the original chord appeared (i.e., if the given chord appeared in the bass notate the transformed chord in the treble clef).

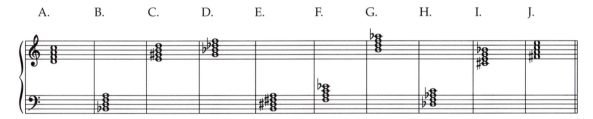

EXERCISE 6.2 Error Detection

A. Below are incorrectly spelled root-position Mm seventh chords. The errors include enharmonic spelling (for example, a Mm seventh built on C must be spelled in thirds: C–E–G–B♭, not C–E–G–A♯) and wrong-note spelling (for example, a Mm seventh built on G is spelled G–B–D–F, not G–B–D–F♯). Correct any errors; there may be one or two. Assume that the root is correct. Renotate each Mm seventh chord up a major third.

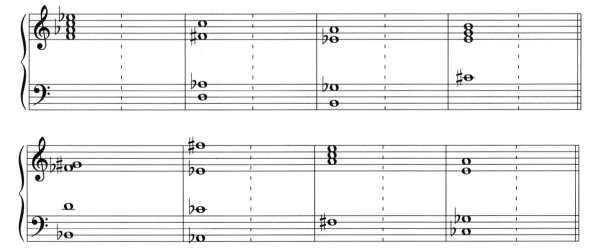

B.   Below are both correctly and incorrectly spelled root-position Mm, mm, MM, dm, and dd seventh chords. If the given sonority is one of the specified seventh chords, assume it is correct and label it. If it is not, correct the notation of the sonority and label its type. There is not more than one error per chord. There may be more than one correct solution for some of the chords; for example, given C♯–E–G♯–B♯, one could create either a dd seventh (C♯–E–G–B♭) or a mm seventh (C♯–E–G♯–B). Transpose each seventh chord down a major third, renotating it in the space provided.

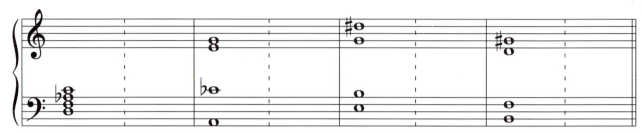

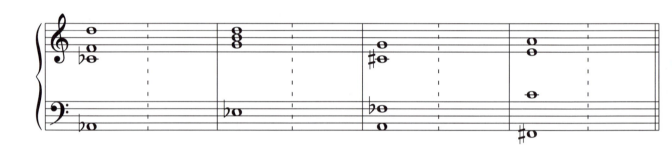

EXERCISE 6.3   Chord Quality Identification and Notation

  You will hear seventh chords of the following qualities: Mm, mm, MM, dm, dd. Based on what you hear, construct root-position seventh chords above the notated roots, first in close position, then in an open position.

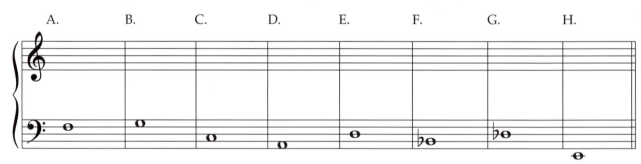

EXERCISE 6.4   Constructing Seventh Chords

  Each of the following pitches is either the root, third, fifth, or seventh of Mm, MM, mm, dm⌀/7, or dd⌀/7 seventh chords. Listen to the given pitch, then to the root-position seventh chord in close position. Label the type of seventh chord and notate the missing three pitches of the seventh chord, making sure that appropriate accidentals appear.

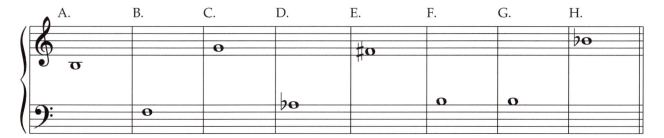

EXERCISE 6.5 Writing More Seventh Chords

A. Write seventh chords given the following:

1. roots of C, E♭, B, write Mm sevenths
2. roots of A♭, F, D, write MM sevenths
3. roots of D, E, A, write mm sevenths
4. roots of C, F, A♭ write dm sevenths
5. roots of B, D, E, write dd sevenths

B. Write the seventh chord in which both given pitches are the specified members:
Sample solution: given: F and D of Mm sevenths:
Answer: B♭: B♭–D–F–A♭ and G: G–B–D–F This answer is deduced as follows: F and D form the interval of a minor third, and in a Mm 7th chord, there is a minor third between the third and the fifth of the chord (i.e., B♭–D–F–A♭) and between the fifth and the seventh of the chord (i.e., G–B–D–F).

1. A♭ and C of MM sevenths
2. C♯ and F♯ MM sevenths
3. B and A of a mm seventh
4. B and D of dd sevenths (consider enharmonic equivalents)

C. Write seventh chords given the following:

1. G is the fifth of Mm seventh
2. F is the fifth of MM seventh
3. A is the seventh of mm seventh
4. B♭ is the fifth of dm seventh

EXERCISE 6.6 Constructing Seventh Chords

You will hear the given pitch followed by an open position seventh chord played in root position. Determine the type of seventh chord and whether the given pitch is the chord's root, third, fifth, or seventh. Notate the missing pitches in close position and label the chord.

EXERCISE 6.7   Error Detection

The pitches of the following seventh chords do not conform to the label beneath them. Renotate the pitches in each given seventh chord so that they conform to the label.

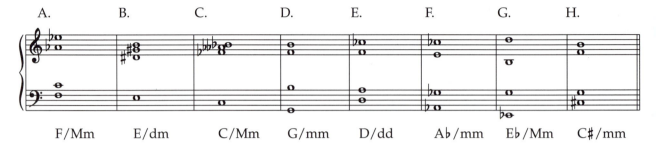

A.   B.   C.   D.   E.   F.   G.   H.

F/Mm   E/dm   C/Mm   G/mm   D/dd   Ab/mm   Eb/Mm   C#/mm

EXERCISE 6.8   Figured Bass: Analysis

Determine the quality of the following seventh chords occurring in root position and inversion and then supply the appropriate full figured bass. (Don't forget to include accidentals.)

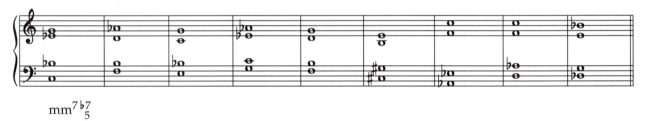

$$mm^{7}{}_{5}^{\flat 7}{}_{\flat}$$

EXERCISE 6.9   Figured Bass: Construction

Realize each of the following figured basses by adding three pitches above each bass pitch in open position, in order to create a 4-part texture. Remember that there are no doublings for seventh chords because they contain four different pitches. Label each type of seventh chord according to its quality (Mm, mm, MM, dm, or dd). Assume that there are no sharps or flats in the key signature.

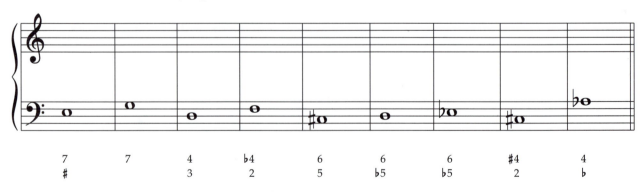

| 7 | 7 | 4 | ♭4 | 6 | 6 | 6 | ♯4 | 4 |
| ♯ | | 3 | 2 | 5 | ♭5 | ♭5 | 2 | ♭ |

EXERCISE 6.10   Analysis: Identification of Seventh Chords in Root Position and Inversion

Below are notated seventh chords that may or may not appear in root position. Listen to and identify the following:

1. The root of the chord.
2. Type of seventh (Mm, MM, mm, dm, dd).
3. What member of the chord (1, 3, 5, 7) appears in the bass? (Give with registral labels.) Provide full figured bass.

	A.	B.	C.	D.	E.	F.	G.	H.
member of chord in bass:	1							
root:	A²							
type of seventh:	mm							
figured bass:	7 5 3							

EXERCISE 6.11   Seventh Chords through the Octave

Write the specified root-position seventh chords. Then renotate the chord at the interval specified. Use enharmonic equivalents for easier notation when you begin to encounter double flats and sharps.

A. major-major seventh chords that begin on F and ascend through major thirds until you return to F

B. major-minor seventh chords that begin on G and ascend through major seconds until you return to G

C. minor-minor seventh chords that begin on A and descend through minor thirds until you return to A

EXERCISE 6.12   Singing Mm Sevenths in Inversion

Given that Mm seventh chords occur far more often than other seventh chords do, you must be familiar not only with their root-position sound, but also with the sound of their inverted forms. Be able to arpeggiate from root position through each inversion until you return to root position. For example, given a B♭ Mm chord, you would sing: B♭–D–F–A♭, D–F–A♭–B♭, F–A♭–B♭–D, A♭–B♭–D–F, B♭–D–F–A♭.

EXERCISE 6.13   Singing Mm and mm Seventh Chords from Given Pitches

Given any pitch, treat it as the root, third, fifth, or seventh of a Mm or mm seventh chord. For example, given the pitch C, treat it as the root of a Mm and mm seventh chord. Then, treat C as the third of a Mm seventh chord (which would be built on A♭) and as the third of a mm seventh chord (which would be built on A). Work at the keyboard in order to check your answers.

EXERCISE 6.14   Aural Identification of Root Position and Inverted Major-Minor Seventh Chords

Listen to and focus on the bass of the following Mm seventh chords that may appear in root position or in any inversion. Then, singing softly, arpeggiate up or down until you find the root and can identify which chord member is in the bass. Indicate the inversion of the chord you hear using figured bass notation.

A. ____   E. ____
B. ____   F. ____
C. ____   G. ____
D. ____   H. ____

EXERCISE 6.15   Figured Bass: Construction

Below is a figured bass that incorporates triads and seventh chords in root position and inversion. Realize each chord according to the figured bass by writing in four voices (thus, for triads you will double the root; there are no doublings for seventh chords, since they contain four different pitches). Then label root and type of each chord. There is no underlying key in this exercise, thus no key signature, so add any necessary accidentals.

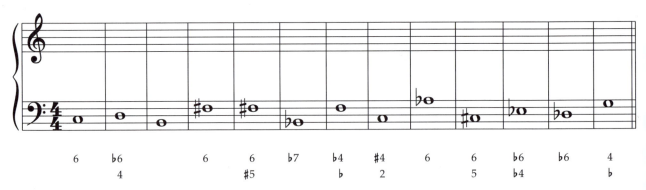

EXERCISE 6.16   Analysis and Error Detection

Notated below are three- and four-note chords in various textures. Listen to each chord, noting whether or not what you hear is what is notated. If it is, write "yes," and label root and chord type. If it is not, write "no" and the correct answer. For example, if a major triad in root position is notated but you hear a minor triad in first inversion, then you would write "no, minor triad, ⁶₃." There is a maximum of one wrong pitch class per chord.

EXERCISE 6.17   Seventh-Chord Completion

 Notated below are incomplete seventh chords: only three voices of their four voices are provided. Listen to each example, which will be played twice: the first time you will hear only the incomplete chords as written; the second time you will hear the complete seventh chord. Notate the missing member(s) of the seventh chord in the correct register (bass = B; tenor = T; alto = A; soprano = S). The five types of seventh chords are Mm, MM, mm, dm, dd; only the Mm will appear in inversion. Analyze each of the seventh chords, identifying the root and the type of seventh, and giving the full figured bass symbols (make sure to show any chromaticism). The first exercise, in which the tenor voice is missing, is completed.

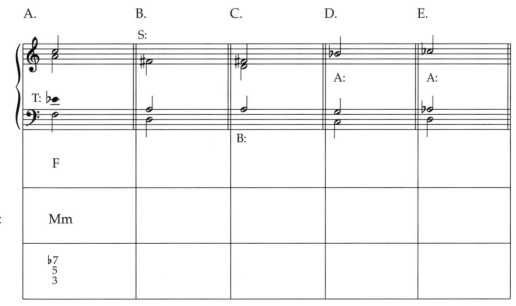

	A.	B.	C.	D.	E.
root:	F				
type of seventh:	Mm				
figured bass:	♭7 5 3				

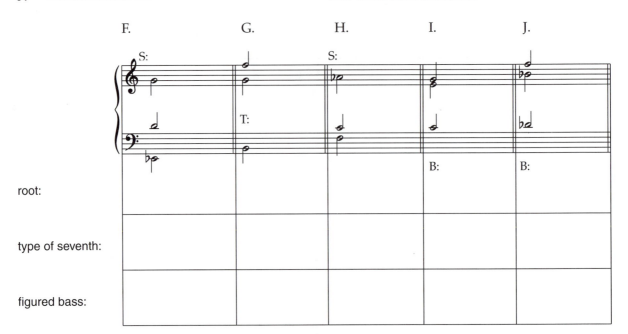

	F.	G.	H.	I.	J.
root:					
type of seventh:					
figured bass:					

EXERCISE 6.18   Analysis

 The point of this exercise is to develop immediate comprehension of triads and seventh chords in various textures. Notes in parentheses are nonchord tones.
Listen to each example and determine:

1. size (triad, seventh chord).
2. root name and quality (for triads: major, minor, and diminished; for seventh chords: Mm, MM, mm, dm, mm). Do not analyze using roman numerals.
3. member of chord in the bass (1, 3, 5, 7).

A.   Tchaikovsky, "Morning Prayer," *Children's Album*, op. 39, no. 1

B.   Corelli, *Adagio*, Concerto Grosso No. 9 in F major, op. 6

C.   Brahms, "Ich stund an einem Morgen" ("One Morning I Stood"), *Deutsche Volkslieder*, WoO 32, no. 9

1. Ich stund an einem Morgen
Heimlich an einem Ort
Da hätt ich mich verborgen,
Ich hört klägliche Wort . . .

2. Herzlieb, ich hab vernommen,
Du wolltst von hinnen schier,
Wenn willst du wiederkommen,
Das sollst du sagen mir; . . .

One morning I stood
secretly in a place
Where I had hidden
I heard the lamenting words . . .

Darling, I have heard
You want to leave here soon.
When will you come back?
Tell me that . . .

D.   Bach, "Christ ist erstanden," Cantata No. 66, *Erfreut euch, ihr Herzen*, BWV 66

E.   Bach, Prelude in C major, *Well-Tempered Clavier*, Book 1, BWV 846

(Continued)

(*Continued*)

F.   Schumann, "Anfangs wollt ich fast verzagen" ("At First I Almost Despaired"),
Liederkreis, op. 24, no. 8

Angfangs wollt' ich fast verzagen,   At first I almost despaired,
und ich glaubt', ich trüg' es nie; . . .   and I thought I would never be able to
                                            bear it; . . .

G.   Debussy: Canope, Preludes, Book 2, no. 10
Analyze only the chords within the boxes.

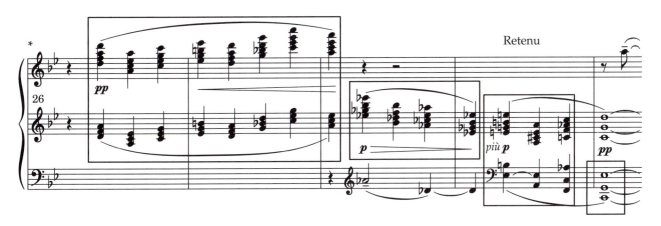

EXERCISE 6.19   Functional Analysis

 Determine the key and provide a roman numeral and figured bass analysis for each chord.

A.   Smart, "Angels from the Realms of Glory"

1. An - gels, from the realms of glo - ry, Wing your flight o'er all the earth;
2. Shep - hers in the field a - Bid - ing, Watch - ing o'er your flocks by night,

B.   Hemy, "There Is a Blessed Home"

1. There is a bless - ed home Be yond - this land of woe,
2. There is a land of peace: Good an gels know it well;

C.   Handel, "The Forsaken Maid's Complaint"
The A that occurs in the vocal line in m. 1 is an accented passing tone.

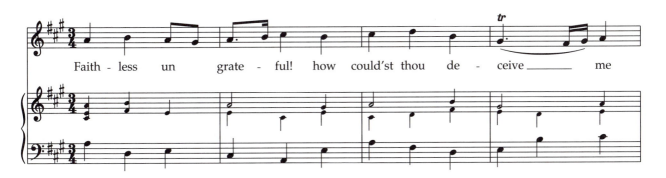

Faith - less un grate - ful! how could'st thou de - ceive _____ me

D.   Bellini, "Sola, furtiva, al tempio" ("Alone, Furtive, to the Temple"), *Norma*, act I, scene vii
Consider the left-hand bass notes to occupy two beats of each measure because they continue to "ring."

Pìu animato

si, __ fa __ co - re e ab - brac - cia - mi. Per - do   no e ti com - pian - go. Dai __

Ah! Sì, fa core e abbracciami.   Ah! Yes, come and embrace me.
Perdono e ti compiango.   I pardon and pity you.

E.   Mozart, *Tema*, Violin Sonata in F major, K. 377

EXERCISE 6.20   Writing Seventh Chords Generated from Scale Degrees

From the information provided, complete the required tasks, which include roman numeral analysis, construction of chords, and adding key signatures.

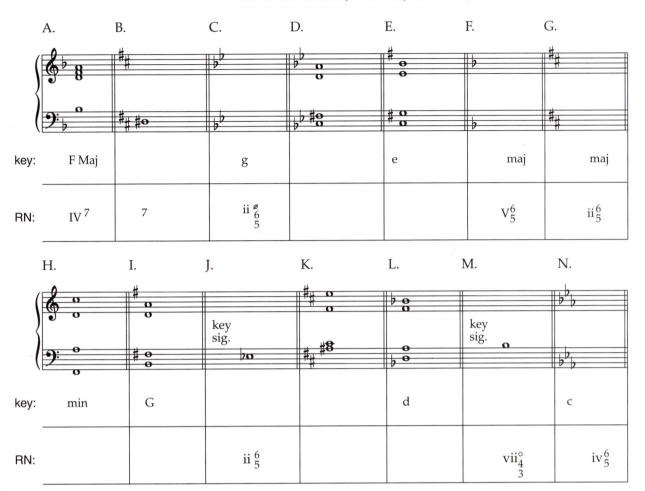

	A.	B.	C.	D.	E.	F.	G.
key:	F Maj		g		e	maj	maj
RN:	IV⁷	7	ii $^{\varnothing}\,^6_5$			V$^6_5$	ii$^6_5$

	H.	I.	J.	K.	L.	M.	N.
key:	min	G			d		c
RN:			ii $^6_5$			vii$^{\circ}{}^6_4{}_3$	iv$^6_5$

EXERCISE 6.21   Singing Seventh Chords from Given Scale Degrees

Choose a major key, play its tonic pitch, and arpeggiate an ascending and descending diatonic seventh chord, which on $\hat{1}$ is a MM seventh chord. Continue singing diatonic seventh chords built on the other diatonic scale degrees in the following manner: arpeggiate the tonic seventh chord again, this time stopping on the seventh of the chord ($\hat{7}$ of the key) and construct the appropriate seventh chord for that scale degree. Continue the process. Do the same for a minor-mode key. Try figuring these seventh chords by inserting either or both neighbor tones and passing tones between the chord members.

EXERCISE 6.22   Harmonic and Melodic Analysis

Analyze, marking the following on the scores. Do not analyze with roman numerals.

1. size of chord (triad or seventh chord)
2. root name and quality (triad: M, m, d; seventh: Mm, MM, mm, dm, dd)
3. member of the chord that is in the bass and soprano (e.g., root, third)
4. label the following tones of figuration in the upper-voice melodies according to these types:
   a. passing tones and whether they are consonant or dissonant: "CPT," "DPT"
   b. neighboring tones and whether they are upper or lower types: "UN," "LN"
   c. chordal leaps: "CL"

A. Haydn, *Adagio*, Piano Sonata No. 53 in E minor, Hob. XVI. 34

B. Mozart, Variation 6, *Variations on "Ah vous dirais-je, Maman,"* K. 265

While the "Twinkle tune" appears in the top of the right hand, the faster figuration notes appear in the bass. Given that the bass provides crucial information that helps us identify harmonies, you will need to distinguish carefully between chord tones and nonchord tones. Circle and label all nonchord tones in the bass as well as the two nonchord tones that appear in the right hand. Ignore the G^5 and F^5 in mm. 3 and 4, marked with parentheses.

C. Chopin, Waltz in B minor, op. posth. 69, no. 2, BI 35

D. Schubert, Waltz in A♯ major, *36 Originaltänze*, op. 9a, D. 365

Like many waltzes, the left-hand downbeat note controls the harmony throughout the measure; consider it sounding even if Schubert has not specified that it be sustained. Ignore notes in parentheses.

E.   Bach, "O Ewigkeit, du Donnerwort" ("O Eternity, You Thunderous Word"), Cantata No. 20, BWV 20

"Open score" refers to a type of notation in which one vocal or instrumental line appears per staff. In the present example, each voice part is arranged from highest (soprano) on the top to lowest (bass) on the bottom. What type of nonchord tone appears in the bass in measure 3 and in the alto in the next measure? Try playing the outer voices together on the piano, then play one of the outer voices while singing the other voice. Ignore notes in parentheses.

O Ewigkeit, du Donnerwort,	O Eternity, you thunderous word
O Schwert, das durch die Seele bohrt,	O sword that bores through the soul,
O Anfang sonder Ende!	O Beginning with no ending!

EXERCISE 6.23   Keyboard: Mm Seventh Chords

Below are three pitches of dominant seventh chords. The root is in the bass. Play the missing member in the right hand with the other two given notes. Return to the beginning of the exercise, play the given voices, then sing the missing voice.

Finally, be able to transpose each chord a major third higher and a perfect fourth lower than written.

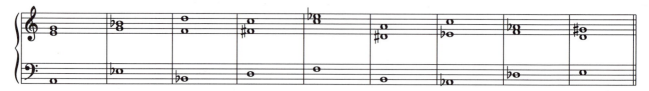

EXERCISE 6.24   Keyboard: More Mm Seventh Chords

Given are three pitches of Mm seventh chords, but the bass may or may not be the chord's root. From the three given pitches, determine the missing member of a dominant seventh chord and play it in the right hand. Play the right-hand notes in two different spacings; an example is given below. Return to the beginning of the exercise, play the given voices, then sing the missing voice. Determine the key of each example (consider the given chord to be V_7 in that key).

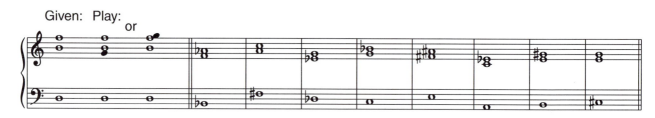

EXERCISE 6.25   Keyboard: Figured Bass and Seventh Chords

Construct seventh chords in keyboard style according to the figured bass. Watch accidentals. Identify the quality of each seventh chord and inversions. There is no underlying key in this example. Transpose each chord down a major third and up a perfect fourth.

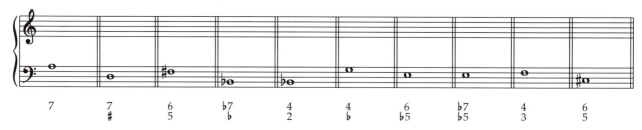

EXERCISE 6.26   Two-Voice Counterpoint: Sing and Play

Playing the given bass pitches with the left hand, create two-voice counterpoint by playing the required intervals above bass. Then, be able to sing one of the voices while playing the other. Be able to play each exercise in the parallel minor and transpose each to one other key of your choice. Part A contains first-species counterpoint and part B contains second-species counterpoint.

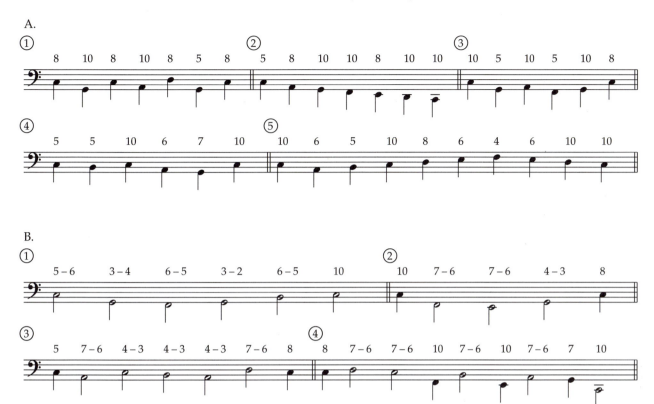

CHAPTER 7

The Tonic and the Dominant, Voice Leading, and Harmonic Rhythm

EXERCISE 7.1 Warm-up for Metrical Hearing (Review)

Before we explore the interaction of harmony and meter, we review metrical patterns. In our dictations, we focus on three meters: $\frac{3}{4}$, $\frac{4}{4}$, and $\frac{6}{8}$. (We will also encounter $\frac{2}{4}$, $\frac{2}{2}$, $\frac{9}{8}$, and $\frac{12}{8}$ in analysis and writing.) The meters $\frac{3}{4}$ and $\frac{4}{4}$ are easily distinguished. The meter $\frac{6}{8}$ is a compound meter: it subdivides the beat into threes, rather than into the twos of $\frac{3}{4}$ and $\frac{4}{4}$. Listen to the following excerpts from the literature and identify a probable meter and an appropriate tempo indication that would correspond to that meter. For example, if you hear the following patterns:

two possible meters are a fast $\frac{4}{4}$ (or $\frac{2}{4}$) (as notated above), or a slow $\frac{4}{4}$, notated thusly:

Your tempo indications are *andante* (slowish, walking), *allegro* (fast), and *molto allegro* (very fast).

	Meter	tempo			Meter	tempo
A.	_____	_____		E.	_____	_____
B.	_____	_____		F.	_____	_____
C.	_____	_____		G.	_____	_____
D.	_____	_____				

EXERCISE 7.2 Identification of Tonic

Below are chord progressions that employ numerous diatonic chords. Label only tonic (I or i) harmonies in the appropriate box; leave remaining boxes blank. Each exercise is in a different key; you will hear I–V–I in the appropriate key to orient you. It is best to sing the tonic triad softly before listening to the exercise.

A. $\frac{4}{4}$: __ __ __ __ | __ __ ___ |

B. $\frac{4}{4}$: __ | __ __ __ __ | __ __ ___ |

C. $\frac{4}{4}$: __ __ __ __ | __ __ __ __ |

D. $\frac{4}{4}$: __ __ __ __ | ___ __ __ |

E. $\frac{3}{4}$: ___ __ | ___ __ | ___ __ | _____ | ___ __ | _____ | _____ |

EXERCISE 7.3   Identification of Tonic and Dominant

Once again, you will hear progressions that use numerous diatonic chords. Label only the I (or i) and V chord, using roman numerals.

A. $\frac{4}{4}$: __ __ __ __ | ____ ____ | __ __ __ __ | _____ |

B. $\frac{3}{4}$: __ | __ __ __ __ | ____ __ | ____ __ | _____ |

C. $\frac{4}{4}$: ____ ____ | ____ ____ | ____ ____ | _____ |

D. $\frac{4}{4}$: ____ ____ | __ __ __ __ | ____ ____ | _____ |

E. $\frac{6}{8}$: ____ __ _____ | ____ __ _____ | ____ __ __ | _____ |

EXERCISE 7.4   Differentiation between I and V

Listen to the following progressions that employ only tonic and dominant chords in root position. Vertical slashes represent bar lines and note values represent durations of harmonies, below which you will write either I or V to indicate the sounding harmony. Be aware that the same harmony may be repeated in different spacings. The first four are in D major; the second four are in B minor. The first one has been done for you.

EXERCISE 7.5 Analysis

Each literature example below contains not only tonic and dominant harmonies, but also other harmonies. In each exercise, label the following:

1. key.
2. only root-position tonic and dominant harmonies (use roman numerals). (An occasional seventh may be added to the dominant; you may ignore it for now.) Many harmonies are to be left unlabeled at this point.
3. the type of cadence that closes each excerpt.

A. Foster, "Jeanie with the Light Brown Hair" Label tones of figuration in the vocal line.

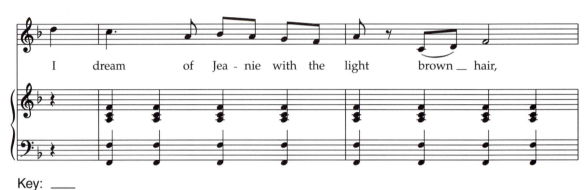

Key: ___

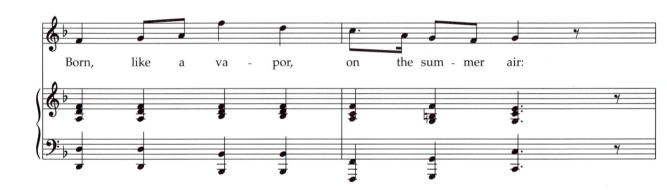

B. Couperin, L'Amphibie, *Pièces de Clavecin Book IV*, 24e Ordre.

C. Corelli, *Vivace,* Concerto Grosso in G minor, "Christmas Concerto," op. 6, no. 8

EXERCISE 7.6   Identification of Tonic and Dominant from the Literature

Label only tonic and dominant harmonies in the appropriate spaces below, ignoring any other diatonic harmonies.

A.   Schubert, "Frühlingstraum" ("A Dream of Springtime"), *Winterreise,* D. 911, no. 11

m.: 1   2   3   4

$^6_8$: ____ | ____ | __ __ | ____ |

B.   Handel, "Air" Concerto Grosso No. 10 in D minor, op. 6, HWV 328

m.: 1   2   3   4

$^3_4$: ____ __ | ____ | __ __ __ | ____ |

C.   Schubert, Impromptu in A♭ , *Six Moments musicaux,* op. 94, D. 780

m.: 1   2   3   4   5   6   7   8

$^3_4$: ____ | ____ | ____ | ____ | ____ | ____ | ____ | ____ |

D.   Chopin, Mazurka in G minor, op. 67, no. 2

m.: 1   2   3   4   5   6

$^3_4$: ____ | ____ | ____ | ____ | ____ | ____ |

E.   Schubert, Waltz in A major, *17 Ländler,* D. 366

m.: 1   2   3   4   5   6   7   8

$^3_4$: ____ | ____ | ____ | ____ | ____ | ____ | ____ | ____ |

EXERCISE 7.7   Analysis

Determine the following for the chord progressions below:

1.   whether the harmony is tonic or dominant (use roman numerals)
2.   whether close (C) or open position (O) is used
3.   which note is doubled (circle the doubled pitch class and indicate whether it is the root, third, or fifth (1, 3, and 5)

A.

B.

EXERCISE 7.8 Error Detection Involving I and V

Examples A–F each contain one error (it is either an error in construction [e.g., missing chordal member, poor spacing, incorrect doubling], voice leading, or part writing [e.g., parallels, direct intervals, nonresolution of tendency tones, and so forth]). Examples G–L contain multiple errors. Identify and label the key; label and circle each error.

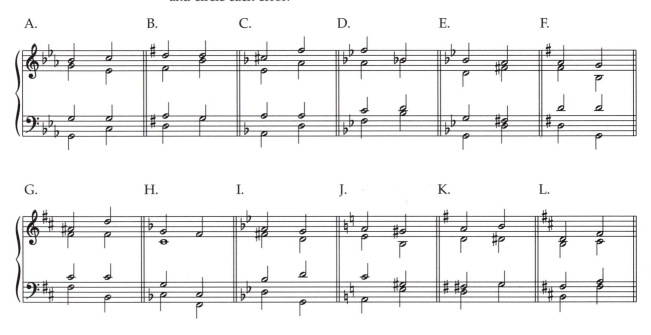

EXERCISE 7.9 Error Detection

Analyze key and roman numerals. Then label chord construction and voice-leading errors in the two examples below. Only tonic and dominant occur. A worked example is given that includes a shorthand labeling system you should use.
Sample:

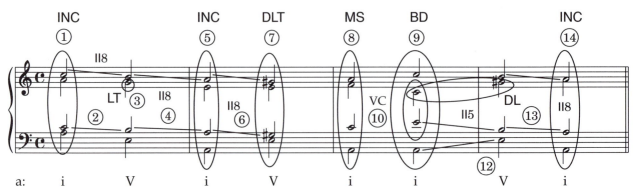

1. An incomplete chord (INC) is a poor way to begin (the fifth—the only chordal member that is permitted to be absent—is missing). The only time that you may use an incomplete chord is when it creates smoother voice leading.
2. Tenor-soprano parallel octaves (P8, with parallel lines showing which voices are involved and the pitches that create the parallels).
3. $\hat{7}$ must be raised to create a leading tone (LT). In minor, you must add this chromaticism to the pitch.
4. Tenor-soprano parallel octaves.
5. No third in tonic chord (BD, for bad doubling) (remember, only the fifth may be absent in a chord).
6. The parallel octaves continue in tenor and soprano.
7. Double leading tone (DLT).
8. Misspelled tonic harmony: F is not a member of the chord (MS).
9. Doubled third for no reason; in fact, it creates problems (see number 10). Remember, you may double anything (except for dissonant notes or the leading tone), since smooth voice leading is the goal, but keep in mind that doubled roots are most common, with doubled fifths next most common.
10. Voice crossing (VC).
11. Difficult, dissonant leap in alto (DL).
12. Contrary (antiparallel) fifths (C^5, with contrary-motion lines showing voices involved).
13. Parallels between soprano and tenor.
14. Four roots and no third or fifth.

A.

B.

EXERCISE 7.10   Completion of Missing Voices

Determine the key and add roman numerals to the incomplete tonic and dominant triads. Then, decide which voice(s) is/are missing and the appropriate chordal member in order to create an SATB texture. Discuss the harmonic rhythm.

EXERCISE 7.11   Completion of Missing Voices

Determine which voice is missing in the examples below. Then, add the appropriate pitches to create a four-voice (SATB) texture. Use only root-position tonic and dominant triads. Double the root. Analyze using roman numerals.

A.

B.

EXERCISE 7.12   Part-Writing Tonic and Dominant in Major

In C major, notate in a meter of your choice the following soprano scale degrees: $\hat{1}$–$\hat{7}$–$\hat{1}$, $\hat{1}$–$\hat{2}$–$\hat{3}$, $\hat{3}$–$\hat{2}$–$\hat{1}$. Then, add a bass line that implies only tonic and dominant triads in root position. Finally, fill in the alto and tenor voices to create a four-voice chorale texture (remember that stems go up for soprano and tenor and down for alto and bass). Analyze and then transpose to the keys of F and A major.

EXERCISE 7.13   Part-Writing Tonic and Dominant in Minor

Using the soprano scale degrees in Exercise 7.12, harmonize using only i–V–i in C minor. Remember that in minor the dominant triad is major, so $\hat{7}$ must be raised via accidental to create a leading tone. Transpose to G and B minor.

EXERCISE 7.14   Part-Writing Progressions

Below are two chord progressions: I–V–V–I and i–i–V–i. Above the progressions are various soprano melodic fragments that can be harmonized by the progression that is given beneath. Choose a meter and a rhythmic setting for the soprano fragments. The final scale degree, harmonized by the tonic, must appear on a downbeat. Notate the outer-voice counterpoint. Then add inner voices, analyze, and label cadences.

Major mode:

A. $\hat{1}$ $\hat{7}$, $\hat{2}$ $\hat{3}$ (in F and D)
    I   V   V   I

B. $\hat{3}$ $\hat{2}$, $\hat{7}$ $\hat{1}$ (in G and E♭)
    I   V   V   I

C. $\hat{1}$ $\hat{7}$, $\hat{2}$ $\hat{1}$ (in B♭ and A)
    I   V   V   I

    $\hat{1}$ $\hat{2}$, $\hat{7}$ $\hat{1}$ (in E and B)
    I   V   V   I

Minor mode:

D. $\hat{1}$ $\hat{3}$, $\hat{2}$ $\hat{3}$ (in d and b)
    i   i   V   i

E. $\hat{3}$ $\hat{1}$, $\hat{2}$ $\hat{3}$ (in c and f♯)
    i   i   V   i

EXERCISE 7.15   Harmonizing Cadential Soprano Progressions

Choose a meter, then write four-voice cadential progressions using only root-position tonic and dominant harmonies based on these soprano fragments. Your order of composition should be: bass line, then alto and tenor lines. Analyze with roman numerals and label the cadence.

A. $\hat{3}$ $\hat{2}$ $\hat{1}$ $\hat{7}$ $\hat{1}$ (D minor, B minor)
B. $\hat{1}$ $\hat{7}$ $\hat{1}$ $\hat{2}$ $\hat{3}$ (A♭ major, E major, C minor)
C. $\hat{1}$ $\hat{2}$ $\hat{3}$ $\hat{5}$ $\hat{5}$ (F major, B♭ major, C♯ minor)

EXERCISE 7.16   Figured Bass

Realize the following figured basses in four voices (SATB), including roman numerals. Change the upper-voice spacings for any repeated bass notes (or octaves).

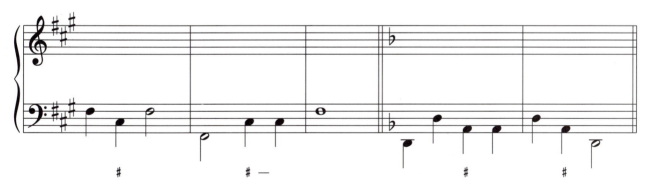

EXERCISE 7.17   Dictation

Notate the bass and soprano voices. Next, provide roman numerals for each chord and identify the type of cadence for the following homophonic progressions. All exercises have two flats. Observe the following steps:

1. Listen to the entire exercise, notating the first harmony and final cadence.
2. Listen for individual chords, focusing on soprano steps and leaps.
3. Check your final product.
    A. Are there any missing notes?

B. Are there any contradictions between harmony and melody? For example, remember that a dominant harmony cannot support $\hat{3}$ in the melody and that it is important to use the leading tone (that is, raised $\hat{7}$, whether it is sharped or naturaled) in minor.

EXERCISE 7.18   Unfigured Bass and Soprano

Realize, then analyze the unfigured bass. There are some submetrical passing tones included. Figured basses are the first steps in understanding harmony because they prescribe harmonic content precisely. That is, you have no choice in the chords that you will write. Unfigured basses are much more challenging, since a given bass note can be harmonized by more than one harmony (e.g., any bass note could be the root, third, or fifth of a triad). Thus, unfigured basses require mastery of the most typical and logical harmonic progressions, and they will regularly occur in the following chapters. An intermediate step between figured bass and unfigured bass is the unfigured bass with a given soprano, since the soprano restricts considerably your chord choice. Thus, begin an unfigured bass with soprano by studying the bass line in conjunction with the soprano, which provides valuable hints in chord choice. Look for cadences and short melodic patterns that have harmonic settings that you have learned. Assiduously avoid vertical "third stacking," in which you haphazardly choose harmonies based on individual bass pitches. Only after you have grouped bass and soprano pitches into logical musical units should you begin to add inner voices and roman numerals. This exercise contains a few submetrical passing tones.

EXERCISE 7.19   Dictation from the Literature

Listen to the following literature excerpts that employ only I and V. Notate the single controlling bass pitch for each measure. Provide roman numerals (when you encounter an accompanimental figure, focus on the lowest-sounding pitch, since it determines the harmony).

A.   B.

C.

D.

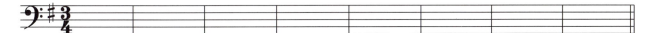

E.   F.

EXERCISE 7.20   Dictation and Second-Level Analysis

Notate the bass and the soprano lines and provide roman numerals for the following homophonic examples. Then, step back in order to determine which harmonies within a measure are more important than others by focusing on the metrical placement of harmonies and the contour of the soprano line. Finally, based on these decisions, bracket entire measures in the bass and provide a second-level analysis in which a single roman numeral represents the underlying harmony that controls each measure. Note that the penultimate measure often contains two harmonies, such as I followed by V, which leads to a final tonic.

A.

B.

C.

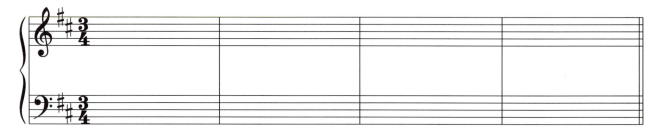

D.

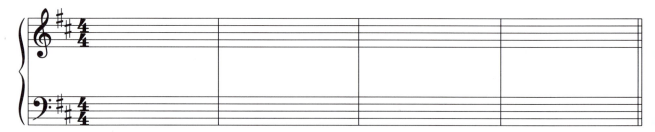

E.

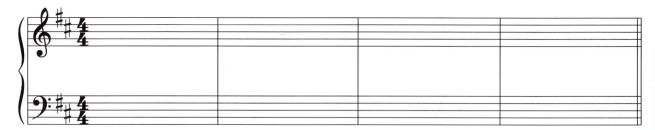

EXERCISE 7.21 Keyboard: Soprano Harmonization

In keyboard style, harmonize each pitch of the following soprano fragments. Use only root-position I and V chords. Except for $\hat{5}$, you will have no choice in the chord you use. Play as written in both major and parallel minor, and transpose to F and D major and minor.

A.   B.

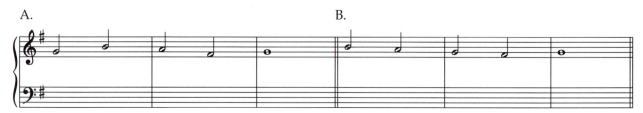

C.   D.

EXERCISE 7.22   Keyboard: Bass Line Harmonization

Play a soprano in note-against-note style that works with the given bass and harmonize using only I and V chords in root position. Then add inner voices (played along with the soprano in the right hand). Revoice right-hand chords when the bass leaps an octave. Transpose the bass to D major and add a different soprano melody and inner voices.

EXERCISE 7.23   Keyboard: Soprano Harmonization

Add a bass line to the soprano melody using only I and V harmonies in root position. Then, add tenor and alto. Transpose to F major. Be able to sing either outer voice while playing the remaining three.

CHAPTER 8

The Dominant Seventh and Chordal Dissonance

EXERCISE 8.1 Analysis of I, V, and V7

1. Label each tonic and dominant harmony. Distinguish between V and V7.
2. Specify whether the sevenths are prepared (not a requirement) and indicate resolution by an arrow (a requirement). If the seventh appears in the top voice, consider the possibility that it might be part of a longer, slower-moving structural line that spans the entire melody, in which case it occurs at the supermetrical level. Remember, the seventh is resolved only by a change of harmony.

A. Haydn, *Scherzo*, Sonatina No. 4, Hob. XVI. 9

There are two appearances of V7; does V7 resolve traditionally both times? Even though the seventh is not prepared by an adjacent pitch, one can argue that it is indeed prepared. Discuss. (Hint: Think at the supermetrical level.)

B. Schumann, "In der Fremde" ("In Foreign Lands"), *Liederkreis*, op. 39, no. 1

Bli - tzen roth da kom - men die Wol - ken her.

Aus der Heimat hinter den Blitzen rot

Da kommen die Wolken her,

From the direction of home, behind
the red flashes of lightning

There come clouds,

C. Chopin, Mazurka in B♭ major, op. 17, no. 1, BI 77
The seventh appears not to resolve. Is this really true? (Hint: Is the cadence an
IAC or a PAC?)

D. Mozart, *Allegro assai,* Symphony No. 22 in C major, K. 162
This is the first of several orchestral scores that you will need to negotiate in
this book. Do not panic; the experienced musician employs certain strategies
when first encountering a full orchestral score. He or she will focus on those instruments that are easiest to read and that carry the most important harmonic
and contrapuntal materials. Begin by looking at the strings, which are the back-
bone of the orchestra and which are laid out in string quartet style: cello and
double bass carry the bass and therefore the harmonic underpinning, while the
first violin carries the contrapuntal melody. The viola part is written in the alto
clef.
    You can then look to the woodwinds, which very often double the strings.
High woodwinds (flutes and oboes) share material with the first and second violin parts, and the bassoon is aligned with the cellos and double basses. Occa-
sionally the high woodwinds (flutes and oboes) may have a separate melody from
the upper strings, so examine these parts carefully. Remember, all of the strings
and many of the winds sound as written (though there are exceptions, such as B♭
clarinet and oboe d'amore in A). Most of the brass instruments are transposing
(horns in F sound down a perfect fifth from the notated pitch, and trumpets in B♭
sound a major second lower than written); it is not until the nineteenth century
that they arise as an independent force in the orchestra. In the eighteenth and first
half of the nineteenth centuries, brass instruments generally double other instruments. In this excerpt, Mozart is using brass instruments in C, thus the pitches

you see are the pitches that sound (though horn in C actually sounds one octave lower than written).

E. Mozart, *Allegro*, String Quartet in A major, K. 464

This example contains a supermetrical passing seventh. Label only root-position tonic and dominant harmonies. Then, trace the long three-note line that comprises the preparation of the seventh, the dissonant seventh, and its resolution.

EXERCISE 8.2   Error Detection

The following four-voice progressions that include root position I V, and V7 contain errors in partwriting, such as construction (spelling, spacing, doubling, and so forth) and voice-leading (parallels, improper resolution of seventh, and so forth). Label the key of each example, then identify and label each type of error. Focus especially on the following types of errors:

1. incorrect treatment of tendency tones
    a) the chordal seventh ($\hat{4}$) must resolve down by step.
    b) the leading tone ($\hat{7}$) must ascend, unless it occurs in an inner voice.

2. V7 follows V; the use of V after V7 is not allowed, given that V7 intensifies V.

3. Since harmonic rhythm usually aligns with metrical stress, chords should change from metrically weak to metrically strong beats (that is, a new

chord, or at least an intensification of a chord such as V moving to V7, should appear on the following downbeat). Examples A–G each contain a single error. Examples H–M contain two or more errors. Example N contains nothing but errors.

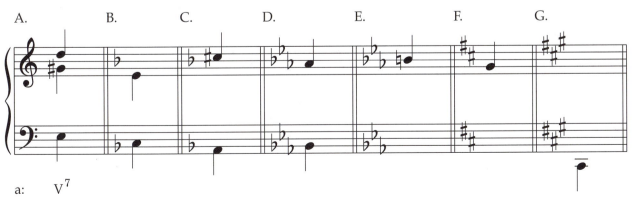

EXERCISE 8.3   Completing V7 in Three and Four Voices

Identify the key and complete the V7 chords below as follows. Examples A–G, in three voices, will be incomplete V_7 chords, (there will be no fifth). Add the missing third or seventh. In examples H–N, add voices to complete the four-voice examples. In these examples, there may be an opportunity either to double the root (and omit the fifth) or to write a complete seventh chord. For Examples H–N, indicate if your chord is complete (C) or incomplete (I). The first one is done for you.

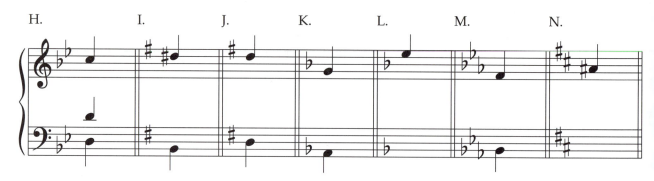

EXERCISE 8.4   Authentic Cadences and Figured Bass

Identify the key for each example, then write authentic cadences in four voices. You may write perfect or imperfect cadences. Specify the type of cadence and analyze with roman numerals. Be sure to obey the voice leading if given by a horizontal dash. The first exercise is completed for you.

EXERCISE 8.5   Writing V7–I Cadences

The following soprano fragments are represented by their scale degrees. Harmonize each in four voices using only I and V in root position; label each cadence and analyze each chord, using roman numerals and figured bass.

A. $\hat{4}$–$\hat{3}$ (D major and relative minor and A major and relative minor)

B. $\hat{2}$–$\hat{1}$ (G major and relative minor and E♭ major and relative minor)

C. $\hat{7}$–$\hat{1}$ (E major and relative minor and B♭ major and relative minor)

D. $\hat{5}$–$\hat{5}$ (C major and relative minor and A♭ and relative minor)

EXERCISE 8.6   More Writing of Root-Position V7

Complete the tasks below in four voices that incorporate root-position V7. Begin by writing note-against-note outer voices; then, fill in tenor and alto. Write at least two different solutions for A and B.

A. Using a passing soprano line, write I–V7–I in D major, F major, E minor, and G minor.

B. Using a neighboring soprano line, write I–V7–I in E major, B♭ major, F♯ minor, and C minor.

EXERCISE 8.7   Analysis and Dictation

The following excerpts do not have bass lines.

A. After listening to each example, notate the missing bass notes.

B. Identify I, V, and V7 using roman numerals.

C. Circle and label any tones of figuration in the melody.

A. Schubert, *Trio*, Minuet in G major, *20 Minuets*, D. 41, no. 20

B. Haydn, German Dance in D major, *Seven German Dances*, Hob. IX. 12

C. Schubert, Waltz in B minor, *38 Waltzes, Ländler, and Ecossaises*, op. 18, no. 6, D. 145

The right-hand G in m. 4 is a dissonant upper neighbor to the harmony's F♯.

D. Haydn, *Allegro*, String Quartet in C major, op. 50, no. 2, Hob. III. 45

EXERCISE 8.8   Harmonization Using V and V7

After choosing a meter, use I, V, and V7 for the soprano fragments below. Remember, the chord progression V to V7 is not reversible. Write each exercise in a different major key and its relative-minor key.

A. $\hat{3}$–$\hat{4}$–$\hat{3}$

B. $\hat{5}$–$\hat{4}$–$\hat{3}$–$\hat{2}$–$\hat{1}$

C. $\hat{1}$–$\hat{7}$–$\hat{1}$–$\hat{2}$–$\hat{4}$–$\hat{3}$

D. $\hat{3}$–$\hat{2}$–$\hat{1}$–$\hat{7}$–$\hat{1}$
E. $\hat{2}$–$\hat{7}$–$\hat{1}$–$\hat{2}$–$\hat{3}$

EXERCISE 8.9 Figured Bass

Realize the two figured basses below in four voices. Write the soprano first, then add tenor and alto. Analyze using two levels; the first level should include every harmonic change, and the second level should prioritize harmonies based on the passing and neighboring motions of the soprano.

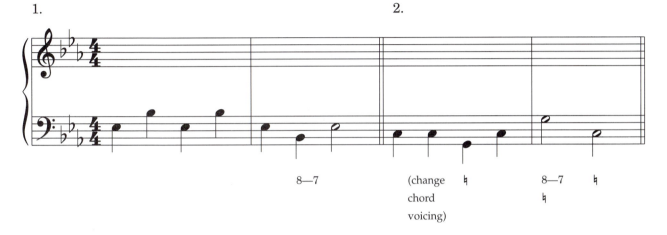

EXERCISE 8.10 Soprano Harmonization

1. Determine whether root position I, V, or V7 chords are implied by the soprano lines below; add roman numerals.
2. Harmonize each soprano pitch with a single bass note to create note-against-note counterpoint.
3. Finally, fill in the alto and tenor voices.

(i)

EXERCISE 8.11 Harmonizing Melodies with Slow Harmonic Rhythm

Determine the key for each exercise below. Sing the melodies in order to determine the appropriate root-position tonic or dominant (seventh) harmonies, then add the root. Most measures will contain a single harmony. Submetrical figuration tones include: chordal skips and leaps, arpeggiations, passing tones, and neighboring tones. Label each.

A.

B.

C.

D.

EXERCISE 8.12 Analysis and Dictation

These incomplete scores from the literature omit the bass lines. You are to do the following:

1. Listen to each example and notate the missing bass notes. Note: In addition to I and V, you may encounter other chords. Listen for their appearance and notate their bass notes only, but do not analyze them.

2. Circle and label tones of figuration in the melody.
A.   Mozart, *Trio II*, Serenade in B♭ major, K. 361

TRIO II

B.   Schumann, "Jemand," *Myrten*, op. 25, no. 4

Mein Herz ist betrübt, ich sag' es nicht,   My heart is distressed, I don't speak
about it,

C.   Schumann, *Scherzo,* String Quartet in A major, op. 41

EXERCISE 8.13   Dictation: Melodies with Accompaniments

 Provide the following on the staves below:

1. key and mode
2. meter
3. number of measures
4. cadence type at close of example
5. bass line and roman numeral analysis

A.

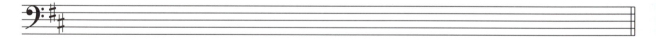

B.

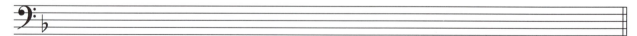

C.   Chopin, Etude, op. 10, no. 3, BI 74

D.   Beethoven, Ecossaise

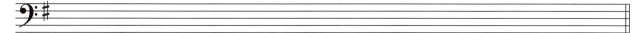

E.   Haydn, String Quartet, op. 64, no. 6, Hob. III. 64

EXERCISE 8.14   Outer Voice Dictation

Notate the bass and soprano voices of the 4-voice homophonic examples. Provide roman numerals.

A.   B.

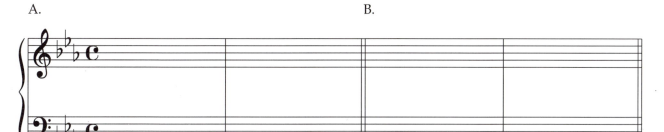

C.   D.

E.

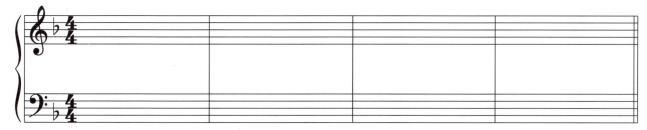

F.

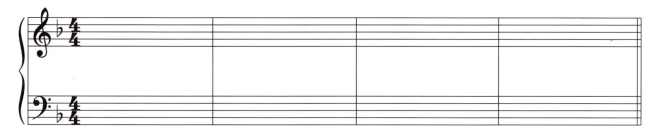

EXERCISE 8.15 Keyboard: Figured Bass

In keyboard style, realize the following figured bass by adding alto and tenor voices. Transpose to a minor key of your choice (except for the parallel minor).

EXERCISE 8.16 Keyboard: Unfigured Bass

Realize the two unfigured basses below in four voices. Analyze with roman numerals.

EXERCISE 8.17 Keyboard: Soprano Harmonization

Choose three soprano melodies and harmonize each pitch by adding the three lower voices. Use only I, V, and V7. Circle all sevenths that occur in the soprano melodies and trace their resolutions. Transpose each melody to one other key of your choice.

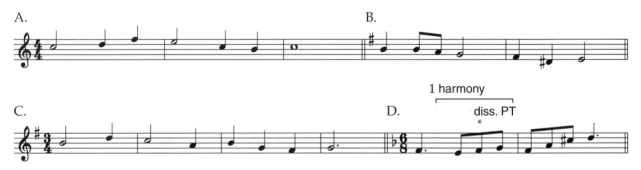

CHAPTER 9

Contrapuntal Expansions of Tonic and Dominant: Six-Three Chords

EXERCISE 9.1   Analysis

Using two levels, analyze the following examples that contain $\frac{5}{3}$ and $\frac{6}{3}$ tonic and dominant triads. The first level is descriptive and provides an analysis of every chord, using roman numerals and figured bass. Level two is interpretive: it identifies what chords are more important than others by using roman numerals for structural chords, and contrapuntal functions (P, N, CS), for expanding harmonies, label cadences. Example A provides a sample solution.

A.   Hasse, *Largo,* Trio Sonata No. 1 in E minor for two flutes and basso continuo

C.

D.   Schubert, "Auf dem Flusse" ("On the Stream"), *Winterreise,* op. 89, no. 7, D. 911
The E in the right hand of m. 3 is a nonchord tone that postpones the following D♯.

Der du so lu - stig rauscht-est,   du   hel - ler, wil - der Fluss,

Der du so lustig rauschtest,   You who rushed so merrily along,
Du heller, wilder Fluss,   You clear, wild stream,

EXERCISE 9.2   Distinguishing between Tonic and Dominant Functions

 Listen to the following examples that contain tonic and dominant triads, their expanding $^6_3$ inversions, and V7 in root position. The meter signature is given and rhythmic values indicate duration. Dashes indicate chord changes. Specify roman numerals and figured bass for each chord. Then, supply a second-level analysis that summarizes the harmony underlying each progression.

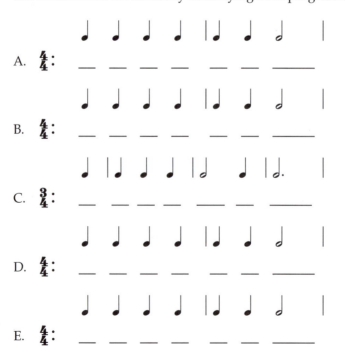

A. **4/4:** ___ ___ ___ ___ ___ ___ ___

B. **4/4:** ___ ___ ___ ___ ___ ___ ___

C. **3/4:** ___ ___ ___ ___ ___ ___ ___

D. **4/4:** ___ ___ ___ ___ ___ ___ ___

E. **4/4:** ___ ___ ___ ___ ___ ___ ___

EXERCISE 9.3 Writing I, I6, V, V7, and V6

Study the soprano fragments to determine a suitable bass line. Begin and end with root-position I and V, but use first inversions when possible inside. Analyze and add inner voices.

in D major, B♭ major, G minor, and E minor: $\hat{3}$–$\hat{1}$–$\hat{7}$–$\hat{1}$
in F major, A♭ major, C minor, and A minor: $\hat{1}$–$\hat{2}$–$\hat{3}$–$\hat{2}$–$\hat{1}$
in G major, A major, F minor, and D minor: $\hat{5}$–$\hat{5}$–$\hat{4}$–$\hat{3}$

EXERCISE 9.4 Figured Bass

1. Study each figured bass, adding a soprano that moves primarily by step and creates mostly imperfect consonances with the bass (that is, thirds and sixths).
2. Analyze, including a second-level analysis, then fill in inner voices.

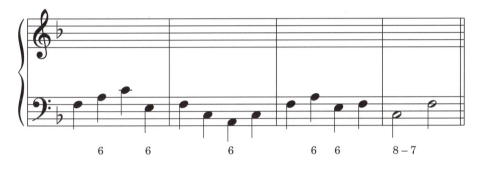

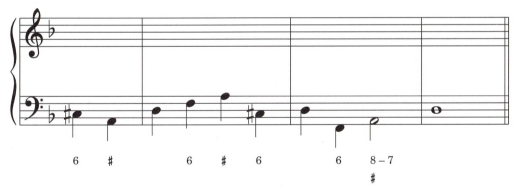

EXERCISE 9.5 Unfigured Bass and Soprano

Determine the implied harmonies in the following unfigured bass. Next, add roman numerals and inner voices as well as a second-level analysis.

EXERCISE 9.6 Notation of I, I6, V, V7, and V6

Listen to, memorize, and notate the bass lines in the following examples and provide a two-level harmonic analysis.

EXERCISE 9.7 Two-Voice Notation and Analysis

1. Listen to the four-voice examples below and notate their outer voices. To do this, listen to the entire example and determine the opening and closing harmonies. Then, start filling in the second level by distinguishing between harmonic progressions and contrapuntal expansions. Finally, memorize and notate one melodic line at a time. (Do not notate individual pitches as they are played; this is an inefficient and dangerous means of taking dictation because the pitches are not within a larger musical context.) A few pitches are provided.
2. Based on the harmonic implications of the outer voices, provide a two-level roman numeral analysis.

A.

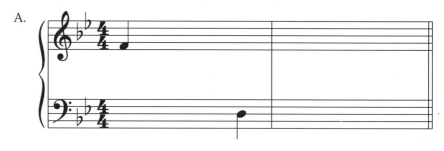

B.

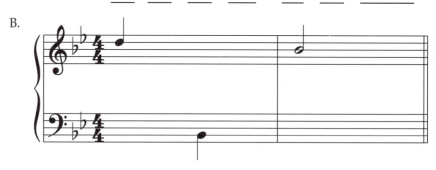

C.

D.

E.

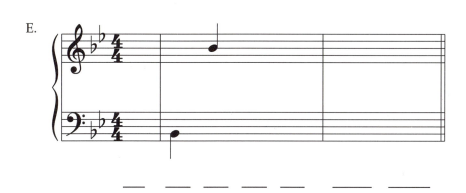

EXERCISE 9.8   Analysis and Dictation

Notate the bass lines and provide a two-level harmonic analysis from the incomplete scores from the literature.

A. Brahms, "Vom verwundeten Knaben" ("Of a Wounded Boy"), op. 14, no. 2

1. Es wollt' ein Mädchen früh aufstehn . . .	A maiden decided to wake up early . . .
2. Und als sie nun in den grünen Wald kam, . . .	And when she came to the green forest, . . .
3. Der Knab', der war von Blut so rot, . . .	The boy, he was so red from blood, . . .

B. Haydn, *Presto,* String Quartet in B minor, op. 64, no. 2, Hob. III. 68

C. Brahms, "Muss es eine Trennung geben" ("Must There Be a Parting"), *Romanzen aus L. Tiecks Magelone* ("Romances from Tieck's Magelone"), op. 33, no. 12
Add eighth-note bass pitches on beats 1 and 4.

Muss es eine Trennung geben,   Must there be a parting
Die das treue Herz zerbricht? . . .   That will cause true hearts to break? . . .

Hör' ich eines Schäfers Flöte,   When I hear a shepherd's flute,
Härme ich mich inniglich, . . .   Inside I grieve; . . .

EXERCISE 9.9 Keyboard: Melody Harmonization

The two melodies below offer the chance to incorporate first-inversion tonic and dominant chords in four-voice keyboard style. Harmonize Example B in both a major key and its relative minor. You may write in two or three bass notes and roman numerals to aid your playing. Be able to sing either outer voice while playing the other three voices.

A.

B.

EXERCISE 9.10 Analysis of Expanded I and V

Your harmonic vocabulary now includes: I, I6, V, V7, V6, and vii°6. Provide a two-level harmonic analysis.

A.   Mozart, *Allegro,* Piano Sonata in B♭ major, K. 281
Two accented nonharmonic tones have been circled in order to help you distinguish chord tones. We will explore such "accented passing tones" in Chapter 11.

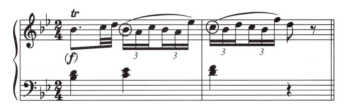

B.   Beethoven, "Freudvoll und leidvoll" ("Joyful and Sorrowful"), op. 84, no. 2
Once again, accented tones of figuration occur on beat 2 of each measure; you need not analyze these for now.

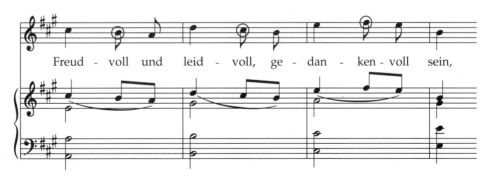

Freud - voll und   leid - voll, ge - dan - ken - voll   sein,

Freudvoll	Joyful
Und leidvoll,	And sorrowful,
Gedankenvoll sein; . . .	Thoughtful; . . .

C.   Vivaldi, *Allegro molto,* Concerto Grosso in G major, op. 9, no. 10, Ry300, Ri125, FI/19, P103

EXERCISE 9.11   Two-Voice Notation and Analysis

You will hear a mix of two-voice and four-voice examples. Notate the pitches of the two-voice examples and the outer voices (soprano and bass) of the four-voice examples. Remember to listen for context and attempt to memorize lines. Analyze with two levels, and the outer voices of the four-voice examples.

A.

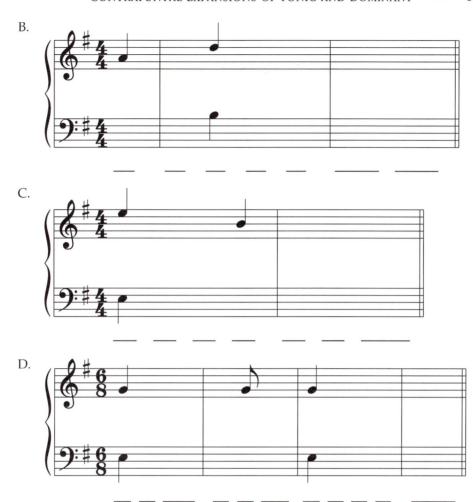

EXERCISE 9.12 Writing IV6

Realize the figured basses in four voices and analyze using two levels.

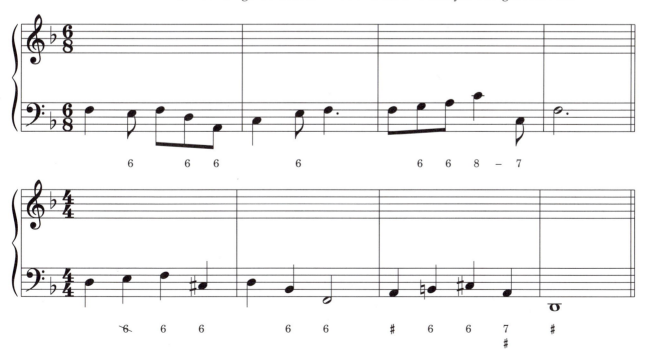

EXERCISE 9.13   Soprano Harmonization

For each soprano fragment, include as many contrapuntal expansions of tonic and dominant as possible. First, study each melody, noting whether I or V controls each measure. Then, write the bass and fill in inner voices. Analyze with two levels, making sure that you have noted all contrapuntal harmonies by their appropriate abbreviation (e.g., N and P).

A.

B.

EXERCISE 9.14   Keyboard: Unfigured Bass

Determine a logical chord progression for the harmonic implications of the unfigured basses below. IV6 and vii°6 are important possibilities. Add inner voices and play in keyboard style. Be able to sing either outer voice while playing the remaining three voices.

A.

B.

EXERCISE 9.15   Melody Harmonization

Harmonize the following melody below according to the rhythmic guidelines with a single harmony per measure, except in measures 5 and 7, where you will write two harmonies in each measure. Analyze with RNs. You need add only a single bass note, but make sure that you include a complete roman numeral and figured-bass analysis.

EXERCISE 9.16   Melody Writing Over an Accompaniment

First, analyze the accompaniment's implied harmonies. Continue the accompaniment based on the harmonic implications of the given bass. Then, write a melody.

EXERCISE 9.17   Keyboard: Singing Operatic Excerpts

Sing the following melodies, then realize their figured basses in keyboard style. Finally, combine the two activities and accompany yourself while singing.

A. Handel, *Samson*, act I, scene 2

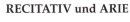

RECITATIV und ARIE

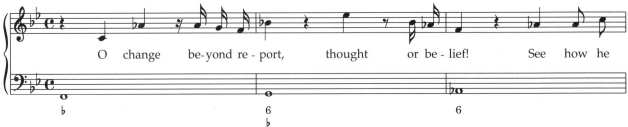

O change be-yond re - port, thought or be - lief! See how he

B. Handel, *Susanna*, act III, scene 2

Hence ev' - ry pang, which late my soul op-press'd com - fort re -

EXERCISE 9.18   Variation and Contrapuntal Expansion of a Harmonic Model

You will now hear contrapuntal expansions of two I–V–I harmonic progressions. Each of the two model bass lines below will be fleshed out in six variations that maintain the metric placement of the given harmonies implied by the bass notes. Complete the following tasks:

1. Notate the bass and soprano voices of the contrapuntal chords that embellish the given harmonic structure.
2. Provide a two-level harmonic analysis. Your harmonic vocabulary now includes: I, I6, IV6, V, V7, V6, and vii°6.

Model #1   Model #2

Var. 1   Var. 1

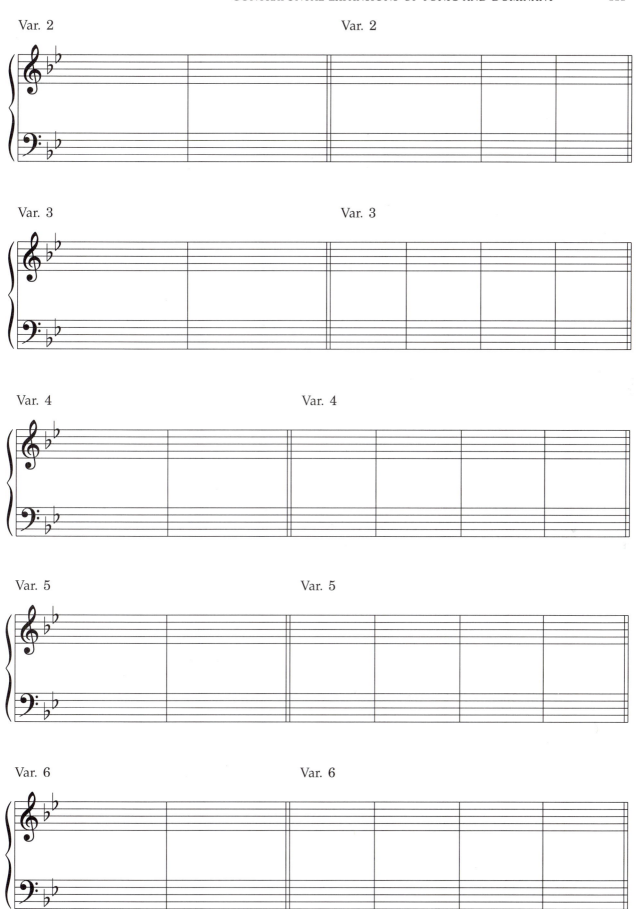

More Contrapuntal Expansions and Their Impact on Composition: Inversions of V₇, and vii°₇, and Introduction of the Motive

EXERCISE 10.1   Analysis

1. Label cadences in the following excerpts, though not every example ends with a cadence. Then provide a first- and second-level analysis.
2. Be on the lookout for chords that may be incomplete. It is possible to determine a chord's identity from its context.

A.   Loeillet, *Second Movement*, Sonata for Oboe in A minor, op. 5, no. 2.

B.   Tchaikovsky, "The Sick Doll," *Children's Pieces*, op. 39

C.   Beethoven, *Largo appassionata*, Piano Sonata No. 2 in A major, op. 2, no. 2

When you do your second-level analysis, focus on m. 3, because it is possible to interpret it as dominant or tonic. Your choice will affect its performance considerably. For example, if you view the dominant to control the measure, the tonic will not be played in a way as to indicate a return to that function; rather, it will sound as if it is harmonizing a soprano passing tone that links statements of the dominant. On the other hand, if you view the tonic as in control, then you might slightly delay and/or intensify through dynamics its return, thus breaking any connection between the preceding and following dominant. Ignore the G♯ that appears in m. 3; it intensifies the motion to the final chord of the excerpt.

D. Beethoven, Rondo, Violin Sonata in D major, op. 12, no. 1.

As in Exercise 10.1C, m. 3 may be variously interpreted as a dominant or tonic in your second-level analysis

E. Schumann, "An meinem Herzen, an meiner Brust" ("At my heart, at my breast"), *Frauenliebe und Leben* ("A Woman's Life and Love"), op. 42, no. 7.

An meinem Herzen, an meiner Brust,
Du meine Wonne, du meine Lust!

At my heart, at my breast,
You are my rapture, my happiness!

F. Brahms, *Andante,* Horn Trio in E♭ major, op. 40

EXERCISE 10.2   Dictation

Notate the bass lines of the following contrapuntal progressions and include a single-level harmonic analysis. Some of the exercises provide a pitch to guide you.

A.   Chopin, Waltz in B minor, op. 69, no. 2, op. posth., BI 95, no. 2

B.   Sammartini, *Allegro*, Recorder Sonata No. 1 in G minor

C.   Beethoven, *Allegro*, Piano Sonata No. 2 in A major, op. 2, no. 2

D.   Beethoven, *Andante*, String Quartet in C# minor, op. 131

E.   Chopin, Nocturne in E minor, op. 72, no. 1, op. posth., BI 11.

F.   Rossini, "Ehi Fiorello," *Il barbiere di Sivigila* ("The Barber of Seville"), act I, scene 3

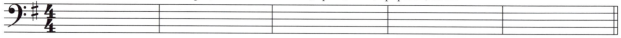

EXERCISE 10.3   Writing Inversions of V7

On a separate sheet of paper, complete the following tasks in four voices and an appropriate meter. Each of the two solutions for A, B, and C should be different.

Play your solutions, being able to sing the bass voice while playing the upper voices.

A.   In D major and A minor, expand tonic using V$^6_5$ as a neighbor

B.   In F major and D minor, expand tonic using a passing V$^4_3$; close with a PAC

C.   In G major and F♯ minor, expand tonic using an incomplete neighboring V$^4_2$; close with a HC

EXERCISE 10.4   Writing Inversions of V7

Using only inversions of V7 to expand the tonic, find a suitable meter and rhythmic setting (based on the criterion that expanding harmonies be placed on weak beats) and write the given soprano or bass line. Add roman numerals and include a second-level analysis. Add the inner voices.

A.   given, the following soprano line in A major: $\hat{3}$–$\hat{4}$–$\hat{3}$–$\hat{1}$–$\hat{7}$–$\hat{1}$–$\hat{1}$–$\hat{2}$–$\hat{3}$–$\hat{5}$–$\hat{4}$–$\hat{3}$–$\hat{3}$–$\hat{2}$–$\hat{4}$–$\hat{3}$

B.   given, the following bass line in B minor: $\hat{1}$–$\hat{7}$–$\hat{1}$–$\hat{1}$–$\hat{4}$–$\hat{3}$–$\hat{1}$–$\hat{2}$–$\hat{3}$–$\hat{1}$–$\hat{3}$–$\hat{2}$–$\hat{7}$–$\hat{1}$

EXERCISE 10.5   Inversions of V7 and Figured Bass

Realize the following figured basses in four voices and provide a two-level harmonic analysis.

A.

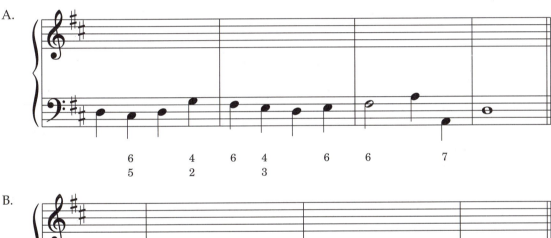

B.

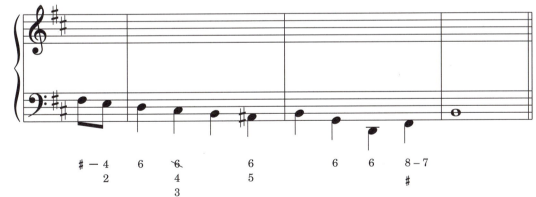

EXERCISE 10.6   Keyboard: Voicing Inverted Dominant
Seventh Chords

Below are right-hand voicings for root-position and inverted dominant seventh chords in F major. Note that root position is the only form that contains four voicings. The inverted forms have only three, because root-position seventh chords may omit the fifth and double the root. Inverted seventh chords, however, must be complete; angled brackets illustrate the "gap" that occurs between various voicings because the missing note occurs in the bass. Transpose to keys up to and including four sharps and four flats.

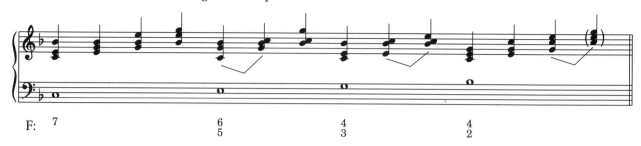

EXERCISE 10.7   Analysis and Dictation of Progressions Using Inversions of V7

 Listen to each of the examples below and notate their bass lines. Include a two-level harmonic analysis.

A.   B.

C.   D.

E.

EXERCISE 10.8   Dictation of Contrapuntal Expansions

Each of the examples contains contrapuntal expansions of I and V. Notate the bass and provide a first-level roman numeral analysis. The chords available are: I, I6, IV6, V, V7, $\frac{6}{5}$, $\frac{4}{3}$, $\frac{4}{2}$, and vii°6.

Listening guidelines: Begin by listening to the entire example, focusing on the large musical context (opening harmony, general shape of melody and the underlying harmonies, and final cadence). Then, in the second and third playings, focus on complete smaller units, such as a two-measure tonic expansion and the chords involved. Use the fourth playing to check your work and fine-tune your harmonic choices (e.g., if $\hat{2}$ occurs in the bass, determine whether it is V$_3^4$ or vii°6). Do not worry if you are still having trouble distinguishing between V6 and V$_5^6$ or vii°6 and V$_3^4$; these are details; it is sufficient to perceive the underlying contrapuntal function and notate the correct bass note.

A.   B.

C.   D.

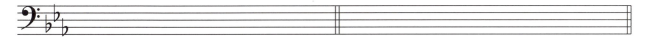

EXERCISE 10.9   Dictation

You will hear eight short progressions, each containing from three to five chords. They are not presented in a metric or rhythmic context. On a separate sheet of manuscript paper, notate only the outer voices and provide roman numerals. Try to memorize each exercise in one or two hearings. All examples contain one flat in their key signatures.

EXERCISE 10.10   Dictation of Figurated Examples

The chords in this exercise are presented as horizontal melodies, and you must combine the members of each chord, aurally stacking them to create a vertical harmonic structure. Notate the bass. Focus on the "sonic dimension" in this exercise rather than the outer-voice counterpoint. That is, listen not only for underlying tonic or dominant progressions but exactly how they are expanded in time.

A.   B.

C.   D.

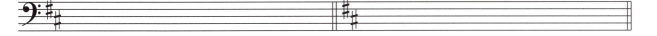

EXERCISE 10.11   Keyboard: Figured Bass and
Contrapuntal Expansions

1. Realize the figured bass in keyboard style.
2. Analyze each expansion and sing either outer voice while playing the other three voices.

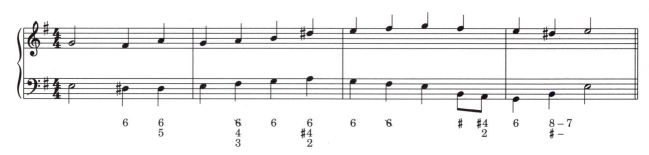

EXERCISE 10.12   Singing vii°7

Using solfège or numbers, sing the following minor-key patterns that contain vii°7.

A.

B.   C.

EXERCISE 10.13   Analysis

Using two levels, analyze the examples below that contain the vii°7 chord. Label preparation and resolution of the seventh.

A.   Mozart, *Allegro*, Piano Sonata in F major, K. 332.
In what key is this passage?

B.   Mozart, *Allegro assai*, Piano Sonata in F major, K. 332.
In what key is this passage?

C.   Beethoven, *Allegro,* Piano Sonata No. 5 in C minor, op. 10, no. 1
Metrically accented dissonances occur in the right hand in mm. 14–16. The chord
tones occur one beat later, as shown by the diagonal lines. Such "suspensions"
are taken up in Chapter 11.

D.   Gluck, Orphee, act I, no. 1 (closing section)

(Continued)

(*Continued*)

press up - on him;   Come, then, come, set him free from dis - tress.
a - mo - ro - sa   tor - to - rel - la a-mo - ro - sa per - dè.

press up - on him;   Come, then, come, set him free from dis - tress.
a - mo - ro - sa   tor - to - rel - la a-mo - ro - sa per - dè.

press up - on him;   Come, then, come, set him free from dis - tress.
a - mo - ro - sa   tor - to - rel - la a-mo - ro - sa per - dè.

press up - on him;   Come, then, come, set him free from dis - tress.
a - mo - ro - sa   tor - to - rel - la a-mo - ro - sa per - dè.

EXERCISE 10.14 Keyboard: Progression Incorporating vii°7

Play the two-measure progression that incorporates vii°7. Transpose it by ascending perfect fourths and continue through C minor. Part of the first transposition is given. Sing bass or soprano while playing.

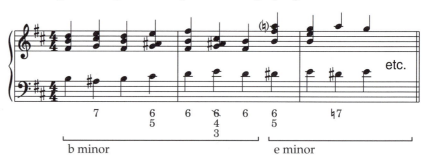

EXERCISE 10.15 Analysis and Dictation

Below are examples in which tonic is expanded by V7 and vii°7; analyze. Listen to the recording, which may or may not play what is notated. If what you hear is what you analyzed, then write "OK." If, however, there are discrepancies between the notated score and what you hear, correct the analysis to reflect the played version.

C.   D.

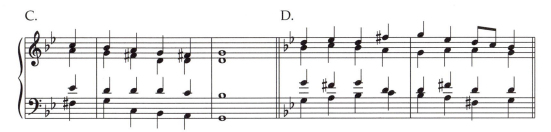

E.

EXERCISE 10.16   Dictation of vii°7

 You will hear examples that use vii°7. Notate the outer voices of exercises A–C and provide roman numerals. Exercises D–H, from the literature, are more figurated; notate only the bass voice and analyze.

A.   B.

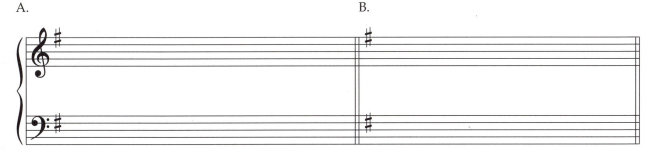

C.   D.   Mozart, *Adagio,* String Quartet in G major, K. 156

E.   Haydn, *Un poco adagio affettuoso,* String Quartet in D major, op. 20, no. 4, Hob. III. 34

F.   Mozart, *Andante,* String Quartet No. 1 in C major, K. 157

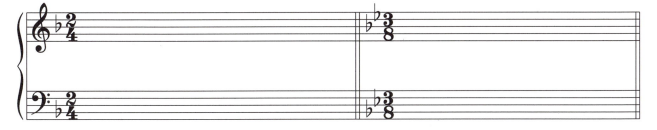

G. Chopin, *Doppio movimento,* Sonata in B♭ minor, op. 35, BI 128

H. Handel, *Allegro,* Concerto Grosso in G minor, op. 6, no. 6, HWV 324

EXERCISE 10.17 Figured Bass

Realize the figured bass below and analyze. Then, add and label unaccented tones of figuration in the upper voices that include: passing tones, neighboring notes, and chordal skips and leaps.

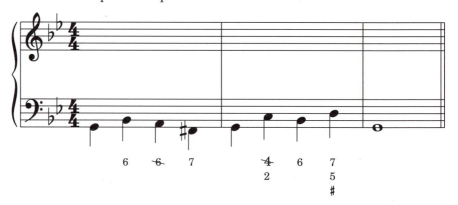

EXERCISE 10.18 Structural Analysis

Provide a two-level harmonic analysis and label cadences. On manuscript paper, extract the two-voice counterpoint that holds together each example. Finally, select one of the excerpts and write a paragraph that describes the motives and their expansions.

A. Handel, *Allegro,* Oboe Concerto in G minor, HWV 287

B. Bach, "Ach Gott, vom Himmel sieh' darein," Cantata 153, *Schall', liever Gott,* BWV 153

Schau' lieber Gott, wie meine Feind' . . .   Behold, O Lord, the many foes . . .
So listig und so mächtig seind, . . .   'Gainst many and such mighty
woes . . .

C.   Beethoven, Piano Sonata No. 14 in C♯ minor ("Moonlight"), op. 27, no. 2

D.   Beethoven, "Ich liebe dich" ("I Love You"), WoO 123

   1.   Describe the melodic motive that appears in each measure of the vocal
        line.
   2.   Make a structural analysis of the vocal line that prioritizes what you be-
        lieve to be the single most important pitch in each measure.
   3.   Based on your structural analysis above, what four-note motive occurs
        over the entire excerpt? Does it relate to your bass line?

Ich lie - be dich, so   wie   du mich, am   A - bend und am Mor - gen,

Ich liebe dich, so wie du mich,   I love you as you love me,
Am Abend und am Morgen, . . .   in the evening and the morning, . . .

EXERCISE 10.19   Writing Harmonic Cells

There are many ways to expand the tonic and dominant. In the following exercise, combine a number of these cells in a logical manner such that you will create a larger four- to eight-measure musical unit.

A.   Choose a key, mode, meter, and a basic rhythmic pattern. For example, in $\frac{6}{8}$,
the pattern quarter-eighth or dotted eighth-sixteenth is very common, so you
might wish to restrict your rhythmic vocabulary to those two patterns in order
to maintain rhythmic consistency.

B.   Provide a general harmonic sketch. You may wish to make a list of various
types of expansions and progressions. For example, a good way to get from I to
I6 is by passing (use vii°6 or V$^4_3$), neighboring (V$^4_2$), or even arpeggiating (use IV6
and arpeggiate down to I6).

C.   Sketch out harmonies beginning with the cadence. If you envision a longer
example, one that encompasses eight measures, then you may wish to subdivide
it into two four-measure units. Thus, the first unit will probably close with a half
cadence.

D.   Focus on individual measures and determine which chord will be the most
important. For example, in $\frac{3}{4}$, you may wish to move from root-position tonic in
the first measure to first inversion in the second measure.

E. Determine local expansions. For example, you may wish to sustain the tonic for two beats in your first $\frac{3}{4}$ measure, and then include a passing chord that links the first-measure tonic with the second-measure first-inversion tonic.

F. Create a soprano melody. You may include submetrical passing and neighboring notes on weak parts of beats. Resolve all dissonance.

G. Add the inner voices; you may include a few nonharmonic tones.

EXERCISE 10.20   Variation and Contrapuntal Expansion of a Harmonic Model

You will now hear contrapuntal expansions of two I–V–I harmonic progressions. Each of the two models below will be fleshed out in variations that maintain the metric placement of the given harmonies. Complete the following tasks:

1. Notate the bass and soprano voices of the contrapuntal chords that embellish the given harmonic structure.
2. Provide a two-level harmonic analysis. Your harmonic vocabulary now includes: I, I6, IV6, V, V6, V7, V$^6_5$, V$^4_3$, V$^4_2$, vii°6, vii°7, vii°$^6_5$, and vii°$^4_3$.

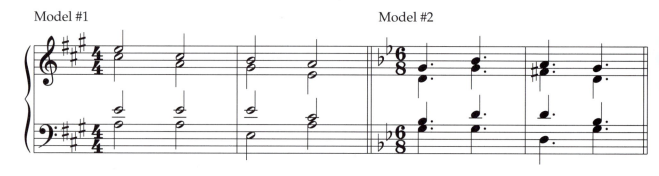

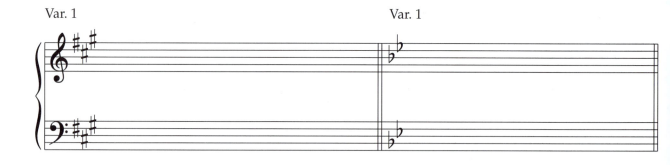

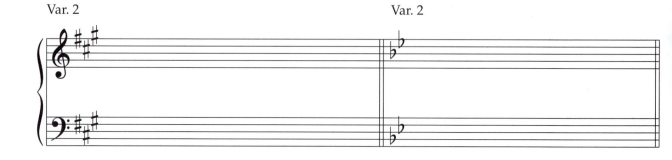

Var. 3

Var. 4

Var. 5

Var. 6

EXERCISE 10.21   Analysis of Implied Harmonies and Motives

Using roman numerals, analyze the following two-voice exercise. Harmonies change twice each measure. Then, using the labeling system presented in m. 1, label recurring melodic gestures. Beware that motives may occupy various levels of the musical structure.

EXERCISE 10.22   Keyboard: Melody Harmonization

Determine a possible key for each of the unmetered melodic fragments below. Then, choose a meter and rhythmic setting and harmonize each in four voices using inversions of V7 to create contrapuntal expansions. You may write out the bass voice.

EXERCISE 10.23   Keyboard: Bass Harmonization

This time you will harmonize bass fragments. Follow the instructions for Exercise 10.22. You may write out the soprano voice.

A.   B.   C.   D.

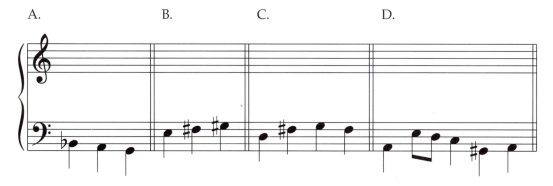

EXERCISE 10.24   Keyboard: Reduction

Play the opening of Haydn's song and analyze it in order to reduce it to a four-voice homophonic texture. Play your four-voice reduction.
Haydn: "Das strickende Mädchen" ("The Knitting Maiden"), *XII Lieder für das Clavier*, Book 1, Hob. XXVIa.1

Phyl - - lis, nicht	der	Vög - lein — sü —	Bes —
herrscht — der Gott	der	Lieb — und — zau -	bert —
man - - ches Jahr	schlich	ich — dir — ein -	sam —

1. "Und hörst du, kleine Phyllis, nicht   "Do you not hear, little Phyllis,
   Der Vöglein süsses Lied? . . . "   The bird's sweet song? . . . "

2. In deinen Augen herrscht   In your eyes rules
   der Gott der Liebe und zaubert . . .   The god of Love and conjures . . .

3. "So manchen Tag, so manches Jahr   "So many days, so many years
   Schlich ich dir einsam nach; . . . "   I wend my way alone . . . "

EXERCISE 10.25   Keyboard: Handel and Kern

Sing the tunes below, then realize the figured bass in keyboard style. Combine the two activities by accompanying yourself as you sing.

A.   Handel, *Semele*, act I, scene 2

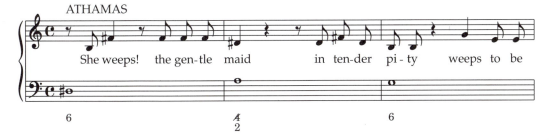

ATHAMAS

She weeps! the gen-tle maid   in ten-der pi - ty   weeps to be

B.   Handel, *Giulio Cesare*, Act 2, scene 2

RECITATIV und ARIE

Ich fühl es wohl   zu mei - nem tief - sten Un - glück,   dass

ihr im Her-zen ra-send schon die Flam-me ent - lo-dert; doch Se - ach-tet,   sie ruft mich auf zur Ra-che.

C.　Kern, "A Fine Romance," *Swing Time*

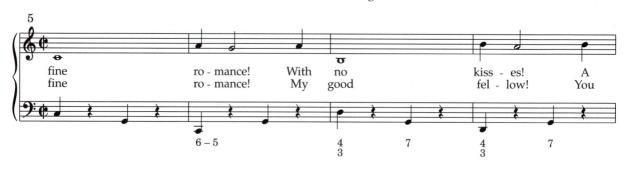

CHAPTER 11

Accented Dissonances, Six-Four Chords, and Revisiting IV

EXERCISE 11.1   Analysis

The following six examples employ both accented and unaccented tones of figuration which may occur in any voice. Begin by providing roman numerals. Then label all tones of figuration according to the text. The chords employed are restricted to those that we have already encountered, except in the cases of suspension chains. For these, simply provide figured bass labels of type 9–8/7–6. Label the components of any suspensions: preparation (P), suspension (S), and resolution (R). Example A has been solved for you.

A.   Haydn, *Presto non troppo,* Piano Sonata No. 50 in D major, Hob. XVI. 37

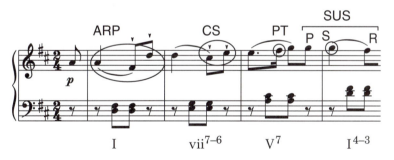

B.   Brahms, "Du mein einzig Licht," *Deutsches Volkslieder,* WoO 33, no. 37

Du mein einzig Licht . . .   You, my only light . . .

129

C.   Loeillet, *Grave,* Sonata in G major for two flutes and basso continuo, op. 1, no. 2

D.   Haydn, *Adagio,* Piano Sonata No. 39 in D major, Hob. XVI. 24

E. Haydn, *Largo*, Piano Sonata No. 11 in B♭ major, Hob. XVI. 2

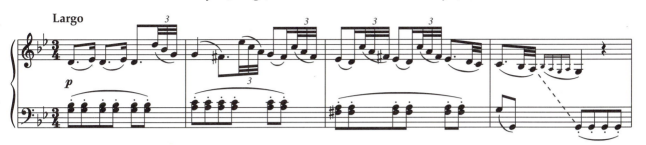

F. Mozart, *Menuetto*, Sonatina in C major, K. 545

EXERCISE 11.2   Suspensions: Error Detection

Label errors in the suspension writing and in the other accented and unaccented figurations, including chord spelling and voice leading. Note: assume that there are no appoggiaturas or anticipations in this exercise. Analyze using two levels of roman numerals. Measures 1–2 in Example A provide a sample solution.

A.

B.

EXERCISE 11.3   Writing Suspensions: Realignment

Analyze the following progressions using two levels. Then, on a separate sheet of manuscript paper, add suspensions to the progressions. The first two measures of Example A are done for you. Given that the resolutions will occur on the weak second and fourth beats, the note values will need to change from half to primarily quarter-note motion. Add one or two suspensions per measure. Hint: Look for descending stepwise motion, then suspend the upper note to create an accented dissonance that will naturally descend. You may also add chordal leaps to prepare the suspensions. These faster notes create another submetrical level of activity, so use them sparingly.

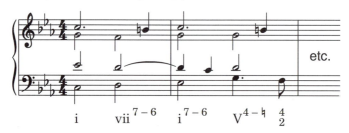

A.

B.

EXERCISE 11.4   Writing Suspensions

Add suspensions according to the given figured bass. When suspensions occur in an outer voice, you must realign the given pitch, since it will be displaced by the suspension. Fill in the inner voices and analyze.

A.

B.

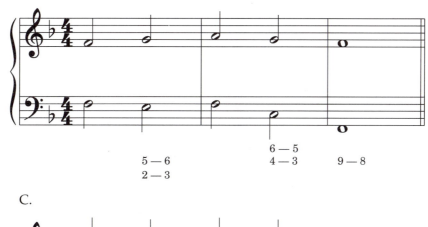

5 — 6
2 — 3
6 — 5
4 — 3
9 — 8

C.

7 — 6   6   7 — 6   4 — 3

D.

7   9 — 8   6 — 5   4 — 3   8 — 7   9 — 8
4 — ♯   4 — ♯

EXERCISE 11.5   Keyboard: Adding Suspensions to Harmonic Cells

Below is a series of harmonic cells in four voices. Play each cell two times, the first time without suspensions, and then, following the figured bass, with the suspensions. Transpose to major and minor keys up to two sharps and two flats.

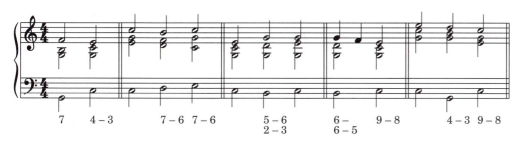

7   4 — 3   7 — 6 7 — 6   5 — 6   6 —   9 — 8   4 — 3 9 — 8
2 — 3   6 — 5

EXERCISE 11.6 Keyboard: Suspensions in a Musical Context

The example below illustrates the most common upper-voice suspensions. Play as written, then transpose to G minor and E minor. Be able to sing either outer voice or the alto while playing the other voices.

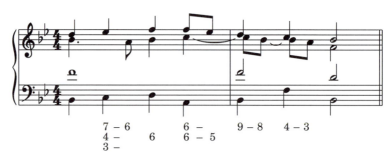

EXERCISE 11.7 Keyboard: Adding Suspensions to a Figured Bass

Realize the following figured bass in four voices. Then, add at least two suspensions in appropriate places. Analyze.

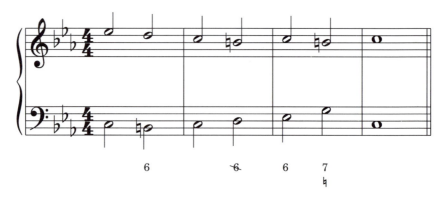

EXERCISE 11.8 Dictation

 On a separate sheet of manuscript paper, notate the outer voices and provide roman numerals for the following examples that incorporate one or two tones of figuration. Label any figurations. The choices are PT (passing tone), CS (chordal skip), APT (accented passing tone), N (neighbor note), SUS (suspension), and APP (appoggiatura).

A.   B.

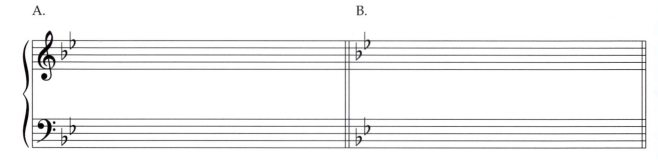

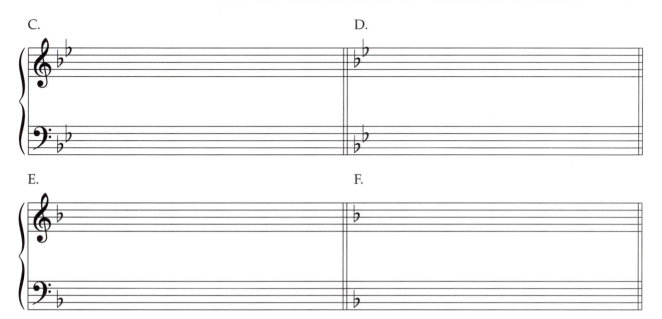

EXERCISE 11.9 Elaborating Homophonic Textures

The excerpts from Bach's chorales below have been stripped of their tones of figuration. Each excerpt appears twice. Add unaccented tones of figuration in the first appearance. These include PT (single and double), NN, CL, and ARP. Add only accented tones of figuration in the chorale's second appearance. These include APT, SUS (single, double, and figurated), and APP. Label each type of figuration. Adhere to the following guidelines:

1. One or two figurations per measure is enough; it is easy to overload the voices with tones that obscure or even contradict the harmony. It is generally safest to avoid any leaping dissonances in the inner voices because they confuse the harmony; reserve such incomplete neighbors, including the appoggiatura, for the soprano, and even then, use them sparingly. The best way to make sure that you have not produced a garish mess is to play your solutions at the piano.

2. It is easy to create problematic parallels when adding passing tones and chordal leaps. Check to make sure you have not fallen into this trap.

A. "Dies sing die heil'gen zehn Gebot," BWV 298

B. "Für Freuden lasst uns springen," BWV 313

C. "Christus, der uns selig macht," *St. John Passion,* BWV 245

EXERCISE 11.10   Writing Tones of Figuration

Complete the following tasks; include roman numeral and figured bass analysis and label each tone of figuration.

A. Set the following melody in four voices in G minor: $\hat{3}$–$\hat{2}$–$\hat{1}$–#$\hat{7}$–$\hat{1}$. Add two suspensions.

B. In F major write a progression that

  1. expands tonic with a voice exchange.
  2. includes a bass suspension.
  3. ends with a PAC and a suspension.

C. In G minor, write a progression that includes at least

  1. one accented passing tone.
  2. one appoggiatura.
  3. one 7–6 suspension.

D. In D minor, write a progression that includes at least

1. one diminished seventh chord that expands the tonic.
2. two different suspension types.
3. one chordal leap and one passing tone.

EXERCISE 11.11   Analysis and Dictation

You will hear embellishments of the homophonic excerpts below. Renotate the scores to reflect what you hear. Exercises A and B contain a maximum of two embellishments. Exercises C–E contain three or more embellishments. Embellishments are PT, CL, APT, NT, SUS, and APP. Begin by analyzing each with roman numerals.

A.   B.

C.

D.

E.

EXERCISE 11.12   Figured Bass

Realize the following figured bass in four voices. Analyze.

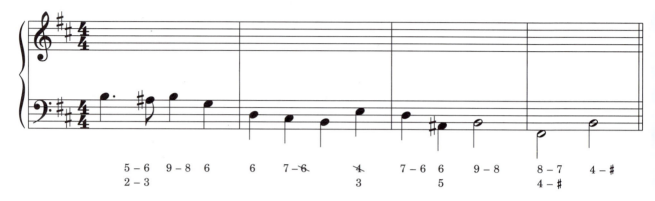

| 5 – 6 | 9 – 8 | 6 | | 6 | 7 – 6 | | ♯ | 7 – 6 | 6 | 9 – 8 | | 8 – 7 | 4 – ♯ |
| 2 – 3 | | | | | | | 3 | | 5 | | | 4 – ♯ | |

EXERCISE 11.13   Dictation

 The following longer examples each contain from two to five tones of figuration. Notate the outer voices and provide roman numerals.

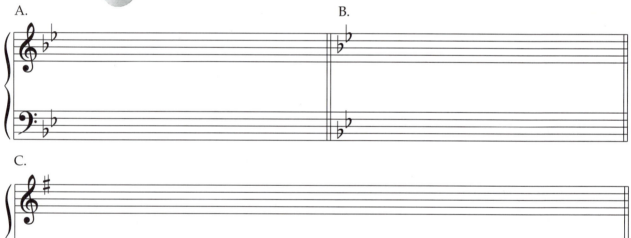

EXERCISE 11.14   Analysis

Analyze the excerpts below with roman numerals and figured bass and label accented tones of figuration.

A.   Bach, "Herr, ich habe missgehandelt," BWV 330

B. Bach, "His Bitter Passion's Story." Be aware that the root (G) appears in the bass at the downbeat of the last measure.

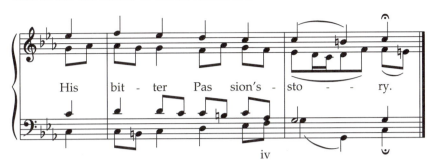

C. Schubert, Waltz in C♯ minor, *36 Originaltänze*, op. 9, D. 365.

EXERCISE 11.15   Unfigured Bass and Melody Harmonization

Determine the best harmonizations for the examples below, using only the chords that we have studied. Add the missing outer voice first. Include a two-level analysis. Add inner voices. Finally, add suspensions and other tones of figuration. You may alter the rhythms in the given voices to include suspensions. In each exercise include and label the following:

1. two different suspensions
2. two unaccented passing tones
3. one accented passing tone
4. one neighbor or appoggiatura

EXERCISE 11.16   Analysis of Six-Four Chords

Listen to each of the following homophonic examples. Provide a two-level roman numeral analysis. Your expanded harmonic vocabulary now includes the following:

- tonic: I, I6
- subdominant: IV6
- dominant V, V6, V7, V $^6_5$, V$^4_3$, V$^4_2$
- dominant substitutes: vii°6; in minor only: vii°7, vii°$^6_5$, vii°$^4_3$
- $^6_4$ chords: passing, neighboring, arpeggiating, pedal, and cadential

A.

B.

C.

D. "Amazing Grace"

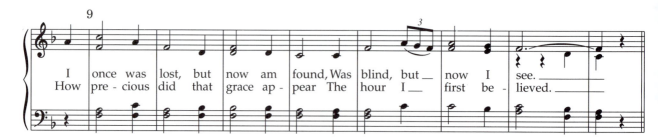

E.   Schumann, "Der Himmel hat eine Träne geweint," op. 37, no. 1

Der Himmel hat ein Träne geweint;   Heaven has shed a tear
Die hat sich in's Meer verlieren gemeint.   That means to lose itself in the sea.

F.   Brahms, *Allegro non troppo*, Symphony 1 in C minor, op. 68

EXERCISE 11.17   Error Detection

Analyze the error-ridden example below with roman numerals and figured bass. Identify errors with numbers keyed to your detailed explanations of what is wrong; errors are not restricted to $^6_4$ chords.

EXERCISE 11.18   Writing $^6_4$ Chords

Harmonize the following sopranos in four voices; analyze. For A, B, and C, include one $^6_4$ chord; for D, E, and F, include at least two. Choose the meters for each example, but be very careful with placement of $^6_4$s!

A. $\hat{3}$–$\hat{2}$–$\hat{1}$ in D minor

B. $\hat{1}$–$\hat{2}$–$\hat{3}$ in B♭ major

C. $\hat{5}$–$\hat{6}$–$\hat{5}$ in A minor

D. $\hat{5}$–$\hat{6}$–$\hat{5}$–$\hat{4}$–$\hat{3}$–$\hat{2}$–$\hat{1}$ in B minor

E. $\hat{5}$–$\hat{5}$–$\hat{5}$–$\hat{4}$–$\hat{3}$–$\hat{2}$–$\hat{1}$–$\hat{1}$–$\hat{7}$–$\hat{1}$ in G major

F. $\hat{1}$–$\hat{2}$–$\hat{3}$–$\hat{4}$–$\hat{5}$–$\hat{6}$–$\hat{5}$–$\hat{3}$–$\hat{2}$–$\hat{1}$ in A major

EXERCISE 11.19 Writing $^6_4$ Chords

Complete the tasks below:

A. In E minor, expand tonic with an N $^6_4$ and end with a PAC that incorporates a Cad. $^6_4$ chord.

B. In E♭ major, expand the tonic with a P $^6_4$ and end with an HC.

C. In G minor, expand the tonic with a iv6; follow this with a P $^6_4$. Complete the progression with a PAC that includes a suspension and a Cad. $^6_4$.

D. In B♭ major, write a four-measure progression that divides into two phrases as follows: close the first half with an HC (use a Cad. $^6_4$); close the second with a PAC. Add one suspension in each phrase.

EXERCISE 11.20 Keyboard: Figured Bass

Realize the figured bass below in four voices. It contains numerous $^6_4$ chords as well as other new devices. Analyze and be able to sing either outer voice while playing the other voices.

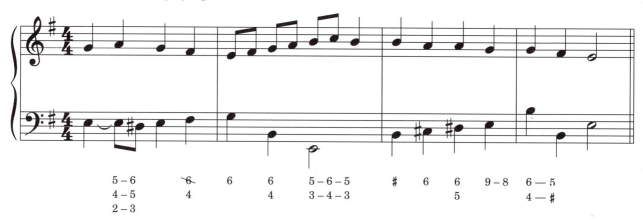

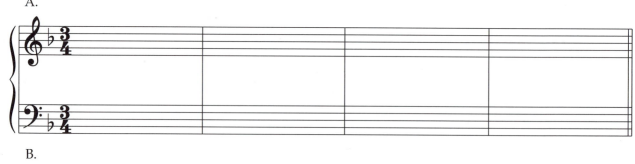

EXERCISE 11.21 Dictation

Notate outer voices and provide a two-level analysis for examples that contain $^6_4$ chords.

A.

B.

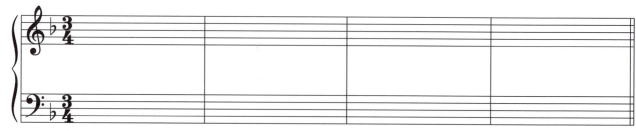

C.

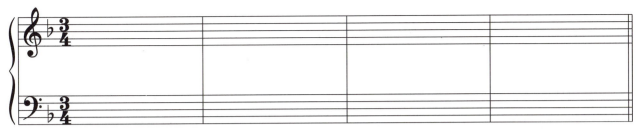

EXERCISE 11.22 Analysis and Dictation

Notate the bass and provide a two-level roman numeral analysis.

A. Fanny Mendelssohn, "Im Wald" ("In the Woods"), *Gartenlieder*, op. 3, no. 6

| Im Wald, im hellen Sonnenschein, | In the woods, in the bright sunshine, |
| wenn alle Knospen . . . | when all the buds . . . |

B. Schubert, "Der Lindenbaum" from *Winterreisse*, op. 89, no. 5, D. 911

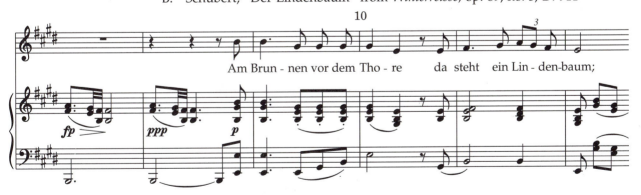

| Am Brunnen vor dem Tore, | By a fountain, near the gate, |
| da steht ein Lindenbaum | There stands a linden tree. |

C. Beethoven, *Adagio*, Piano Sonata No. 1 in F minor, op. 2, no. 1
In what key is this example?

D.   Mozart, "Non ti fidar, o misera" ("Do Not Believe, O Miserable One"), *Don Giovanni*, Act I, scene 12, K. 527

Non ti fidar, o misera,   Do not believe, o miserable one,
Di quel ribaldo cor . . .   In that faithless heart . . .

E. Beethoven, "An die Geliebte" ("To the Beloved"), WoO 140

O dass ich dir vom stillen Auge   O, if only from your quiet eye
In seinem liebevollen Schein   in its love-filled gleam

EXERCISE 11.23   Figured Bass and $^6_4$ Chords

Realize the figured bass below in four voices; analyze with roman numerals.

EXERCISE 11.24 Analysis

Below are excerpts from the literature. Analyze and, in a paragraph, compare and contrast their harmonic, contrapuntal, and motivic structures.

A. Beethoven, *Adagio con molto e cantabile,* Symphony No. 9, op. 125

V_3^4 of V

B. Haydn, *Allegretto,* String Quartet in B♭ major, op. 33, no. 4, Hob. III. 40

C. Beethoven, "La Partenza" ("Der Abscheid," "The Farewell"), WoO 124

Das ist die Schreck-ens stun - de, has mei-ne lip - pen _ be - ben,

EXERCISE 11.25 Analysis

Below are examples in which the subdominant extends tonic. Six-fours are also included. Analyze each example, labeling the function of each subdominant.

A.   Tchaikovsky, "Old French Song," *Children's Album,* op. 3, no. 16

B.   Leclair, *Allegro assai,* Trio Sonata in D major, op. 2, no. 8

C.   "Wayfaring Stranger"

I   am   a   poor _____ way-far-ing   stran-ger, _____ A- trav-'ling

D. Gruber, "Silent Night"

EXERCISE 11.26 Writing the Subdominant

Complete the following tasks:

A. In A minor, expand the tonic twice, both times using the subdominant but in different ways. Close with a plagal cadence.

B. Harmonize the following soprano fragments in E♭ major and E minor; include at least one statement of IV in each example. Consider the harmonic rhythm carefully, given that IV should be metrically unaccented.

1. $\hat{5}$–$\hat{6}$–$\hat{5}$–$\hat{4}$–$\hat{3}$
2. $\hat{3}$–$\hat{2}$–$\hat{1}$–$\hat{1}$–$\hat{1}$
3. $\hat{1}$–$\hat{2}$–$\hat{3}$–$\hat{4}$–$\hat{3}$–$\hat{4}$–$\hat{5}$

C. Realize the following figured bass in four voices; begin by bracketing harmonic cells. Analyze.

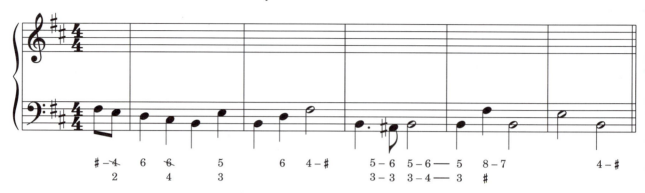

EXERCISE 11.27 Dictation

 You will hear examples in which the subdominant extends the tonic. Notate bass and soprano in Examples A–D, then analyze with roman numerals and figured bass. Notate only the bass and analyze for Examples E–G.

A.

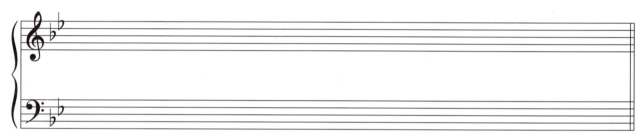

B.

C.

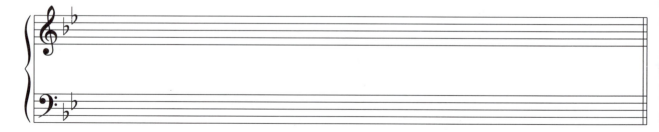

D.

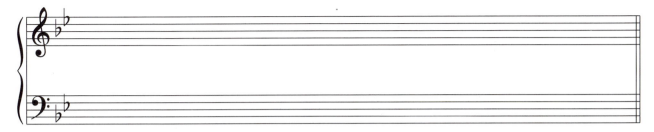

E. Schumann: "Sheherazade," *Album für die Jugend,* op. 68, no. 22

F. "Red River Valley"

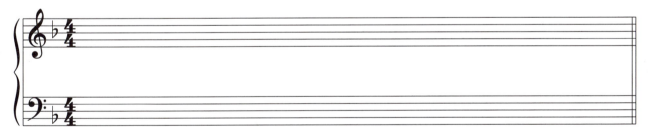

G.

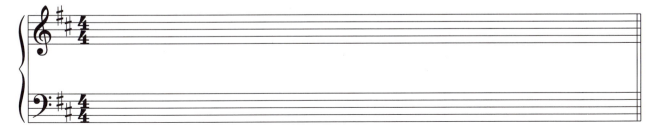

EXERCISE 11.28   Keyboard: Figured Bass

Realize in four voices the figured bass below that incorporates IV in root position. Analyze.

EXERCISE 11.29   Keyboard: Illustrations

In four voices, play the following progressions. You may write out a bass line, but if you do, you must also be able to sing it while playing the other voices.

A.   a progression in E minor, $\frac{4}{4}$, that

1.   expands tonic with a passing $^6_4$ chord.
2.   closes with a cadential $^6_4$ chord and PAC.
3.   contains a 4–3 suspension.

B.   a progression in C minor, $\frac{4}{4}$, that considerably expands the tonic using the following chords in any order:

1.   a diminished seventh chord
2.   a passing V^4_3
3.   a descending bass arpeggiation incorporating iv6

C.   a progression in B minor, $\frac{6}{8}$, that

1.   contains one bass suspension.
2.   contains a passing $^6_4$ chord and one chordal leap.
3.   closes with a cadential $^6_4$ chord.

CHAPTER 12

Invertible Counterpoint and Compound Melody

EXERCISE 12.1   Singing and Playing Invertible Counterpoint

Sing one voice while playing the other in the short exercises below, then swap the pitches in each voice in order to create invertible counterpoint. Then repeat the exercise, this time singing and playing the opposite voices. Determine the implied harmonies in each exercise and play in four voices the original and inverted forms. (Note, that all of these exercises expand the tonic.) Play each example in major and the parallel minor, and transpose to two other keys of your choice. Example A is completed for you.

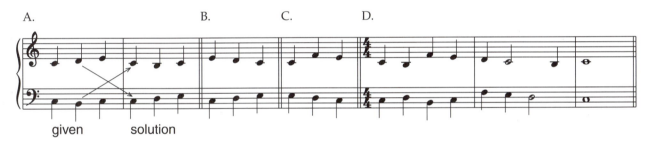

EXERCISE 12.2   Analysis of Compound Melodies

Analyze the underlying harmonies, circling and labeling all nonharmonic tones. When you encounter a harmony that we have not covered, simply write the letter name of the chord's root and its appropriate figured bass.

A.   Next, make a voice-leading representation of the outer voices.

B.   If more than the two outer voices are present, add the inner parts. You need not worry about strict voice leading because inner voices are treated quite freely, sometimes dropping out and reentering the texture.

Example A is completed for you.

B. Chopin, Waltz in B minor, op. 69, no. 2

C. Corelli, *Allegro*, Violin Sonata in B♭ major, op. 5, no. 2

D. Bach, *Giga*, Partita No. 2 for Solo Violin in D minor, BWV 1004

E. Bach, Prelude, Cello Suite No. 2 in D minor, BWV 1008

F. Bach, *Bourree I*, Cello Suite No. 3 in C major, BWV 1009

G.   Bach, *Allemande,* Cello Suite No. 2 in D minor, BWV 1008

H.   Bach, *Gigue,* Cello Suite No. 2 in D minor, BWV 1008

EXERCISE 12.3   Analysis of Incomplete Harmonies

Using roman numerals, analyze the passages based on the harmonic implications of the incomplete chords. Label all tones of figuration, including passing and neighbor tones and suspensions. Note: You will encounter only the chords that we have studied, except for two instances that are labeled.

A.

B.

C.   Bach, *Minuet,* French Suite in B minor, BWV 814

D.   Haydn, *Moderato,* Piano Sonata No. 30 in D major, Hob. XVI. 19

E.   Haydn, *Presto,* Piano Sonata No. 5 in G major, Hob. XVI. 11
What contrapuntal technique is used in mm. 9–12?

EXERCISE 12.4   Composition

Complete the following compound melody excerpt. Begin by studying the given
bass and determining the appropriate harmonies. Next, add the upper voices.
Maintain the basic pattern. Feel free to write a different phrase that ends on a half
cadence, then play the new phrase, followed by the given phrase, creating a larger
antecedent-consequent structure.

CHAPTER 13

The Pre-Dominant Function and the Phrase Model

EXERCISE 13.1   Aural Identification of Pre-dominants

Write the roman numeral of the pre-dominant that occurs in each short example (six to eight chords). Your choices are: ii (root position in major only), ii6 and IV (major and minor modes), and iv6 (in minor only, as part of half cadence).

A. _____
B. _____
C. _____
D. _____
E. _____
F. _____
G. _____
H. _____
I. _____
J. _____
K. _____
L. _____

EXERCISE 13.2   Notation of Pre-dominants

Memorize each progression's basic harmonic structure, focusing on the bass. Then, notate the bass line and provide roman numerals.

A.

B.

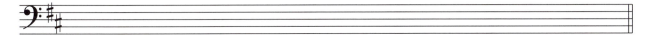

C.

D.

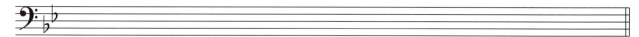

E.

F.

EXERCISE 13.3   Dictation and Analysis

 Examples A–D are homophonic; examples E–G are taken from the literature. The upper voices are given. Notate the bass and provide roman numerals and second-level analysis. Begin by listening to the examples and by studying the harmonic implications of the upper voices.

A.

B.

C.

D.

E.　Haydn, *Menuetto,* String Quartet in G major, op. 76, no. 1, Hob. III. 75

F.　Haydn, *Menuetto,* String Quartet in D major, op. 76, no. 5, Hob. III. 79

G. Beethoven, *Adagio ma non troppo,* String Quartet No. 6 in B♭ major, op. 18, no. 6

EXERCISE 13.4   Error Detection

The following exercise contains a number of voice-leading errors. After providing a roman numeral analysis in two levels, circle and label voice-leading and spelling problems.

EXERCISE 13.5   Pre-dominants and Figured Bass

Realize the following figured basses, first composing the soprano in good counterpoint with the bass, and then adding inner voices. Analyze with two levels. Note: Some IV chords are pre-dominants, while others are contrapuntal or embellishing chords.

A.

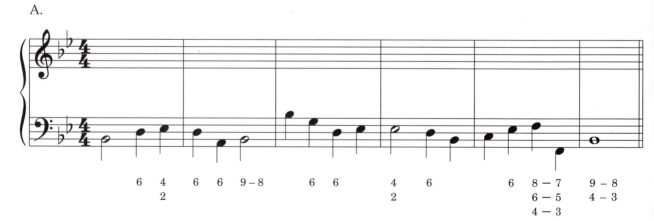

B.

6	6	4 — #	4	6	6	6	6 — 5
5			2		4		4 — #
					3		

6	7 – 6	4	6	7 – 6	6	6	6	8–7	4 – 2 – ♮
4		3		4				#–
			3				

EXERCISE 13.6 Pre-dominant Writing: Multiple Settings of Soprano Fragments

Write three different, logical bass lines for the two soprano fragments. Use the bass staff below for the first and manuscript paper for the other two. Analyze. Extra credit: Add inner voices.

A.

B.

EXERCISE 13.7   Keyboard: Illustrations

Complete the following in four voices:

A. In G minor, establish the key, move to a pre-dominant iv chord, and close with an IAC.

B. In C major, create a progression that contains at least two suspensions and a supertonic chord. End with a half cadence.

C. In A minor, include the following: (1) scale degree bass line $\hat{1}$–$\hat{6}$–$\hat{3}$ to extend the tonic, (2) a ii°6 pre-dominant, and (3) a cadential six-four chord.

D. In B♭ major, include two different six-four chords and a ii chord in root position before closing with a PAC.

EXERCISE 13.8   Homophonic Dictation

Draw five vertical lines, each of which represents one measure in a four-measure phrase model. Listen to the following homophonic examples, and, using roman numerals, label the controlling harmony for each measure or part of measure. Note that the opening tonic usually occupies much more time than the pre-dominant, dominant, and final tonic. Each of the eight example's phrase models unfolds as follows: T-Pd-D-T.

EXERCISE 13.9   Figurated Dictation from the Literature

Using roman numerals, label the underlying harmonic progression in the phrase models. Also, label the cadence type. There is usually one chordal function per measure, though two functions may appear in the same measure.

A. Schumann, "Tief im Herzen trag' ich Pein" ("Deep in My Heart I Suffer"), *Spanisches Liebeslieder (Spanish Love Songs)*, op. 138, no. 2

____ | ____ | ____ | ____ | ____‖

B. Haydn, *Adagio,* Piano Sonata in D major, Hob. XVI. 24

____ | ____ | ____ | ____ | ____ |

C. Haydn, *Menuetto allegretto,* String Quartet in B♭ major, op. 50, no. 6, "Der Frosch," Hob. III. 49

____ | ____ | ____ | ____ | ____‖

D. Haydn, "Die Himmel erzählend die Ehre Gottes" ("The Heavens are Telling"), *Die Schöpfung (The Creation)*, Hob. XXI. 2

____ | ____ | ____ | ____ | ____‖

E. Bach, "Wo soll ich fliehen hin," Cantatas 163 and 148, BWV 153 and 148

____ | ____ | ____ | ____ | ____‖

EXERCISE 13.10   Notation of Bass Lines

Before we turn to methods for memorizing and notating the outer voices of complete phrases, we first notate the bass lines below the given upper voices. Examples A–E are homophonic chord progressions with only a few melodic embellishments. Examples F–I are drawn from the literature. Determine the chords implied by the given voices before listening to the example. Notate the bass and add roman numerals.

A.

B.

C.

D.

E.

F. Schubert, "Litanei auf das Fest Aller Seelen" ("Litany for the Feast of All Souls"), D. 343

1. Ruhn in Frieden alle Seelen, . . .   Rest in peace, all souls . . .
2. Liebvoller Mädchen Seelen . . .   Maiden souls, full of love, . . .
3. Und die nie der Sonne lachten, . . .   And those who never smiled at the sun . . .

G. Loeillet, *Largo,* Trio Sonata in B♭ major, op. 2, no. 9

H. Schumann, "Die beiden Grenadiere" ("The Two Grenadiers"), op. 49, no. 1

So will ich liegen und horchen still,
Wie eine Schildwach, im Grabe,
Bis einst ich höre Kanonengebrüll
Und wiehernder Rosse Getrabe.

So shall I lie and hark in the ground,
A guardwatch, silently staying
Till once more I hear the cannon's pound
And the hoofbeats of horses neighing.

EXERCISE 13.11 Keyboard: Reduction and Improvisation

Play the opening of Couperin's "Les ombres errantes." Then, reduce
Couperin's figurated texture into a homophonic chord progression and play
it in keyboard texture. Play the bass voice one octave lower than written and
follow voice-leading rules. Then, using any of the broken chord or arpeggiating figures that we have encountered before, improvise on this four-voice
structure.

EXERCISE 13.12 Keyboard: Unfigured Basses

Realize the unfigured basses in four-voice keyboard style. Analyze.

A.

B.

EXERCISE 13.13 Removing Flesh from Bones

Each example below represents the fleshing out of a basic contrapuntal progression. Play each example, then reduce the texture to simple four-voice homophony by following these guidelines: determine each measure's governing harmony, omit repeated notes and nonchord tones, and look for a mostly stepwise soprano voice. Play your reduction in four voices. Then check your answers against the first- and second-species reductions that follow the exercise.

A. Andante

B. tempo di valse

C. Allegretto

A1.

B1.

C1.

EXERCISE 13.14   Keyboard: Handel and Beethoven

Sing the tunes from the excerpts below and determine the key of each excerpt. Be aware that the key signature may not reflect the key of the excerpt. Then realize the figured bass in keyboard style. Finally, combine the two activities by accompanying yourself while you sing.

A.   Handel, "My Cup Is Full," *Joshua,* act 3, scene 1

B.   Handel, "Of My Ill-Boding Dream," *Semele,* act 3, scene 8

C. Beethoven, "Mit einem gemalten Band" ("With a Painted Ribbon"), op. 83, no. 3

EXERCISE 13.15 Composition

The phrase below closes with a half cadence. Analyze the remaining harmonies, then write an appropriate consequent phrase that closes on the tonic.

The Phrase Model Continued: Perceiving, Animating, and Expanding It Using New Pre-Dominant Possibilities

EXERCISE 14.1   Dictation

This dictation exercise focuses on notating the outer voices of phrases that include a few given pitches. Listen to each phrase four times. On the first playing, focus on the underlying harmonic progression. Keep the meter in mind, noting the changes from tonic to pre-dominant to dominant within the phrase. Then, add roman numerals and the bass of the harmonic changes that occur after the tonic expansion. After the second playing, notate the bass line for the tonic expansion, and any structural melodic notes (for example, the first pitch and the two or three pitches involved in the cadence). On the third playing, complete the melody. Try to reserve the fourth playing for checking your work.

EXERCISE 14.2 Dictation

Listen to each phrase four times. On the first playing, focus on the underlying harmonic progression. Keep the meter in mind, noting the changes from tonic to pre-dominant to dominant within the phrase. Then, add roman numerals and the bass of the harmonic changes that follow the tonic expansion. On the second playing, notate the rest of the bass line and structural melodic notes. On the third playing, complete the melody. Check your work on the fourth playing.

A.

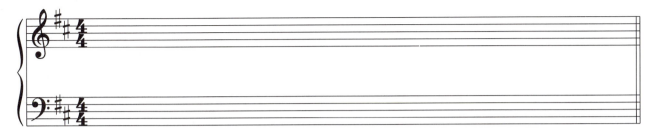

B.

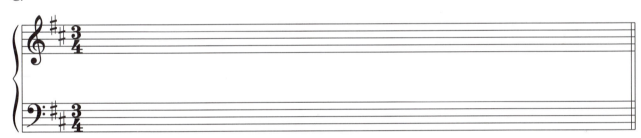

C.

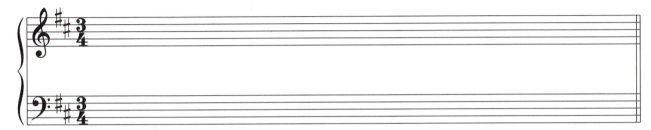

D.

E.

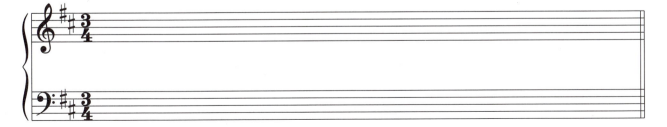

F.

EXERCISE 14.3   Figurated Textures

 This exercise incorporates a melody over a figurated accompaniment. Notate the bass and provide roman numerals.

A.

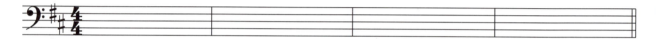

B.

C.

D.

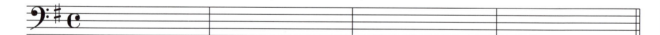

E.

EXERCISE 14.4   Keyboard: Model Progressions Using Pre-dominant Seventh Chords

Play the four-voice models below as written and in major and minor keys up to and including two sharps and two flats. Be able to sing either outer voice while playing the other three voices. Circle the seventh of each pre-dominant seventh chord, then draw a line to its preparation and resolution pitches. Provide roman numerals and figured bass for models C and D.

A.

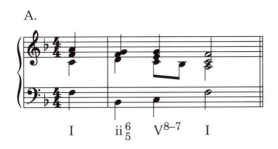

$$\text{I} \qquad \text{ii}^6_5 \qquad \text{V}^{8-7} \qquad \text{I}$$

B.

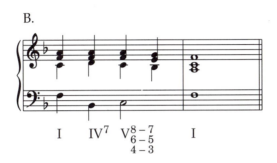

$$\text{I} \qquad \text{IV}^7 \qquad \text{V}^{\substack{8-7\\6-5\\4-3}} \qquad \text{I}$$

C.   D.

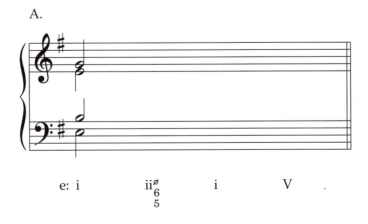

EXERCISE 14.5   Writing and Playing Nondominant Seventh Chords in Context

Complete the progressions below in four voices, then be able to play them on the piano. Transpose each exercise to a different key of your choice.

A.

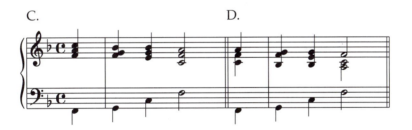

$$\text{e: i} \qquad \text{ii}^{\varnothing\,6}_{\quad\,5} \qquad \text{i} \qquad \text{V}$$

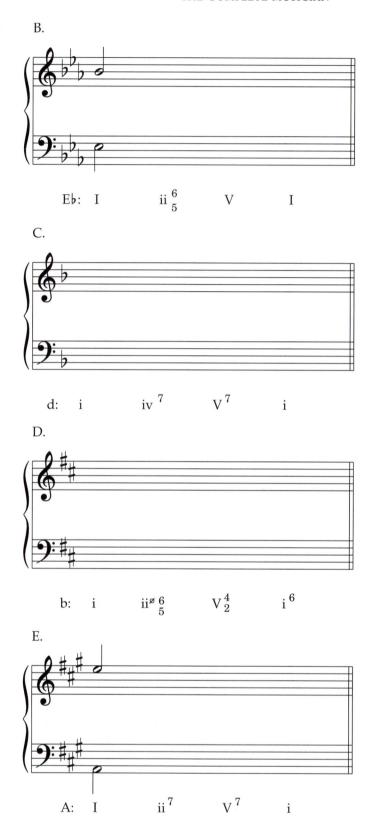

B.

E♭:   I   ii $\frac{6}{5}$ V   I

C.

d: i   iv ^{7} V ^{7} i

D.

b: i   ii^{ø} $\frac{6}{5}$ V $\frac{4}{2}$ i ^{6}

E.

A: I   ii ^{7} V ^{7} i

EXERCISE 14.6   Bass Dictation from the Literature

Notate the bass line and provide roman numerals; focus on the type of nondominant seventh used.

A.   Beethoven, "Rule Britannia," *Fünf Variationen* in D major, WoO 79

B.   Schumann, "Auf einer Burg" ("In a Castle"), *Liederkreis,* op. 39, no. 7

C.   Haydn, *Allegretto,* Piano Sonata in E major, Hob. XVI. 37

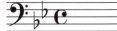

D.   Mozart, "Rex tremendae," *Requiem,* K. 626

E.   Handel, *Adagio,* Chamber Sonata No. 22

EXERCISE 14.7   Writing Embedded Cadential Motions (ECMs) and Contrapuntal Cadences

Complete these tasks and analyze using two levels:

A.   In D minor, write a short progression that contains two tonic expansions, each of which uses a different ECM.

B.   Set the following soprano melody in B minor: $\hat{5}$–$\hat{4}$–$\hat{4}$–$\hat{3}$–$\hat{2}$–$\hat{7}$–$\hat{1}$. Include ii$^4_2$–V$^6_5$.

EXERCISE 14.8   Dictation of Nondominant Seventh Chords

Notate outer voices and provide roman numerals for the examples that contain nondominant sevenths and ECMs.

A.

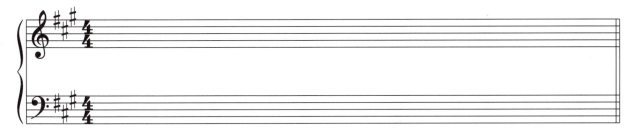

B.

C.

D.

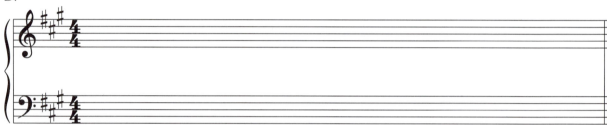

EXERCISE 14.9 Figured Bass

Realize the following figured bass example in four voices. Provide a two-level analysis.

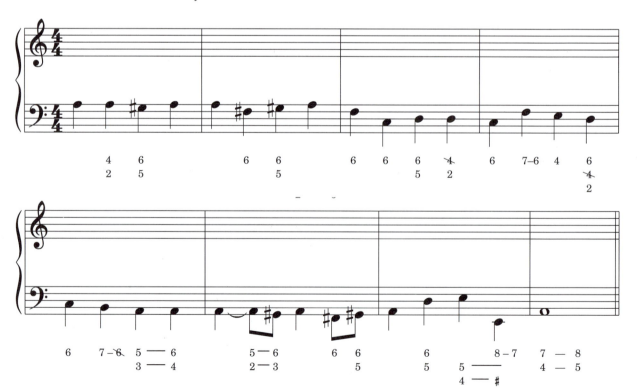

EXERCISE 14.10   Analysis of Expanded Pre-dominant Functions

Analyze the following three excerpts.

1. Determine tonic, pre-dominant, and dominant functions, focusing on expanded pre-dominants.
2. Next, determine how the function is expanded. For example, is there literal repetition, change of inversion, passing or neighboring chords, or ECMs? Label the chords and summarize what occurs in the pre-dominant area.
3. Finally, provide roman numerals for the entire passage.

A.

B.   Mendelssohn, *Lieder ohne Worte* ("Song Without Words"), No. 45 in C major, op. 102

Notice the tonic pedal that occurs in mm. 1 and 2. What harmonic progression is implied above the pedal? Label accordingly.

C.   Mozart, *Menuetto,* Symphony No. 30 in D major, K. 202

EXERCISE 14.11 Variation and Contrapuntal Expansion of a Harmonic Model

You will now hear contrapuntal expansions of two I–Pd–V–I harmonic progressions. Each of the two outer voice models below will be fleshed out in variations that maintain the metric placement of the implied harmonies. Complete the following tasks:

1. Notate the bass and soprano voices of the contrapuntal chords that embellish the given harmonic structure.
2. Provide a two-level harmonic analysis. Your harmonic vocabulary now includes: I, I6, IV6, V, V6, V7, V_5^6, V_3^4, V_2^4, vii°6, vii°7, vii°$_5^6$, and vii°$_3^4$, and pre-dominants: ii, ii6, ii7, ii$_5^6$, ii$_3^4$, IV, IV6, IV7, IV$_5^6$. Don't forget ECMs and contrapuntal cadences.

Model A:

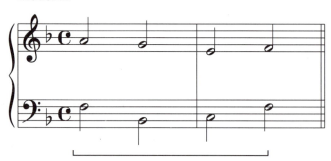

expansions 1 – 2 are 2 measures.
expansions 3 – 4 are 4 measures.

1.   2.

3.

4.

Model B:

expansions 1 – 4 are 2 measures.
expansions 5 – 6 are 4 measures.

1.   2.

3.   4.

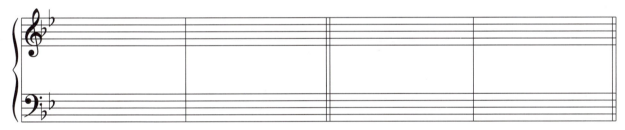

5.

6.

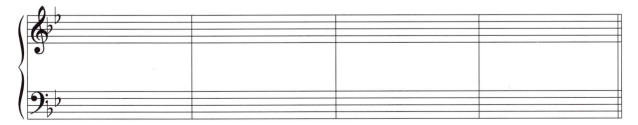

EXERCISE 14.12   Writing Extended Pre-dominants

Complete the following tasks in four voices; provide a two-level analysis.

A. In D major, write a four-measure progression that

    1. expands tonic with an ECM; close with an IAC.
    2. expands the PD at the cadence through voice exchange.
    3. includes at least one suspension.

B. In B minor, write a four-measure progression that

    1. includes a bass suspension.
    2. includes a tonic expansion with a bass that descends a sixth from $\hat{1}$ to $\hat{3}$.
    3. expands the PD with a $^6_4$ chord.
    4. concludes with an IAC.

EXERCISE 14.13   Composition Project

Below are two models, each of which can be fleshed out into a two-phrase musical unit. (Such a musical unit is called a period. We will explore periods in detail in Chapter 17.)

A. Choose, then compose according to one of the models below. Begin with good outer voices in a major key of your choice and label the implied harmonies. Label tonic, pre-dominant, and dominant expansions.

B. Flesh out the texture in four voices and, if you desire, figurate your texture.

C. Elaborate your melody with suspensions, arpeggios, passing notes, and embellishing skips.

D. Along the same lines, elaborate the inner voices appropriately.

mm:	1	2	3	4		5	6	7	8
	I	I	PD–V	IAC		I	I	PD–D(7)	PAC

mm:	1	2	3	4		5	6	7	8
	I	I	I	PD–V (HC)		I	I	PD–D(7)	I (PAC)

EXERCISE 14.14   Phrases and Subphrases

Determine whether the examples below contain single phrases with one or more subphrases, or multiple phrases. Support your answer in one or two sentences. Bracket phrases beneath the bass clef and subphrases above the treble clef. Remember, phrases are self-standing musical units that contain harmonic motion (that is, a traversing of tonic and dominant functions) and that are articulated by a cadence. Subphrases combine to create phrases (usually in proportional pairs) and therefore are subordinate to phrases. Yet, subphrases are in many ways self-standing, given that they may contain miniature harmonic motions (e.g., ECMs) and even weak cadential gestures (e.g., contrapuntal cadences). Be aware that musical flow may come to a stop because of a caesura, but that does not necessarily mean that you have encountered a subphrase. Note that, given the slippery nature of subphrases, there will often be more than one possible interpretation in the examples below.

A. Haydn, *Allegro*, Piano Sonata No. 19 in E minor, Hob. XVI. 47

B. Mozart, "Bei Männern," *Die Zauberflöte (The Magic Flute)*, act I, scene 7, K. 620

Bei Männern, welche Liebe fühlen,	The man who feels love
Fehlt auch ein gutes Herze nicht.	Will also have a good heart.

C. Haydn, "Im holder Arnmut stehn" ("Most Beautiful Appear"), *Die Schöpfung (The Creation)*, part I, no. 19, Hob. XXI. 2

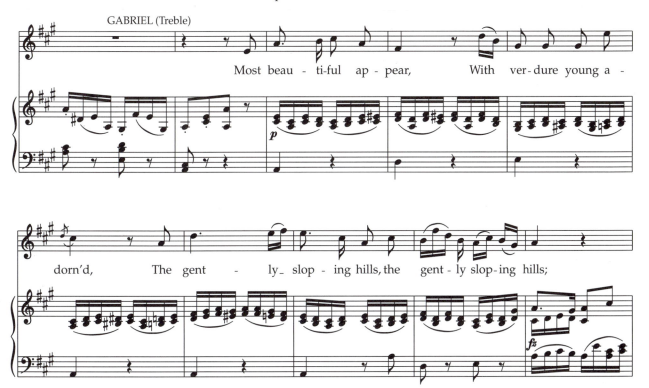

Im holder Anmut stehn	Most beautiful appear,
Mit humgem Grün geschmückt	With verdure young adordn'd,
Die wogigten Hügel da,	The gently sloping hills,

D. Haydn, *Moderato*, Sonata No. 35 in A♭ major, Hob. XVI. 34

E. Beethoven, *Klavierstück*, WoO 82

EXERCISE 14.15   Analysis: Subphrases and Composite Phrases

Analyze each example, determining whether Haydn has created extended phrases through a single large-scale progression or through a series of linked subordinate harmonic motions.

A. Haydn, *Allegretto*, Piano Sonata No. 32 in G minor, Hob. XVI. 44

B. Schubert, "Der Einsame"

Wenn mei-ne Gril-len schwir - ren, bei Nacht, am spät er-wärm-ten   Herd,

dann sitz ich, mit ver-gnüg-tem Sinn, ver-trau-lich zu der Flam-me hin,   dann

sitz ich, mit ver-gnüg-tem Sinn, ver-trau-lich zu der Flam-me hin,

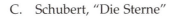

C. Schubert, "Die Sterne"

Wie blit-zen die Ster-ne so hell durch die Nacht!_____

bin oft schon dar-ü-ber vom Schlum-mer er-wacht._____

D.   Haydn, *Presto*, Piano Sonata in E♭ major, Hob. XVI. 52

EXERCISE 14.16   Keyboard: Figured Bass

Realize the figured bass below in four voices. Be able to analyze the progression and to sing either outer voice while playing the three other voices. Bracket and label phrases, subphrases, ECMs, expanded pre-dominants, and contrapuntal cadences.

EXERCISE 14.17   Keyboard: Figured Bass Recitative from Handel

Sing the tune from Handel's *Judas Maccabeus*. You must determine the key from the context, since there is no key signature. Then, realize the figured bass. Finally, be able to accompany your singing with your figured bass realization.

Handel, "Ye Worshippers," *Judas Maccabeus*, act 2, no. 49, HWV 63

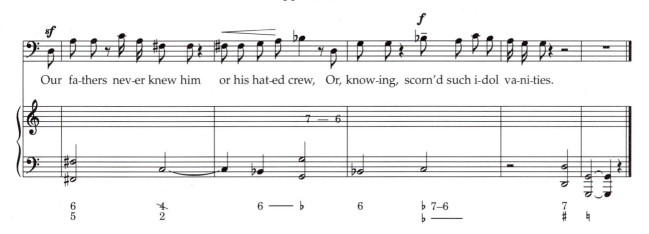

Our fa-thers nev-er knew him   or his hat-ed crew, Or, know-ing, scorn'd such i-dol va-ni-ties.

CHAPTER 15

The Submediant: A New Diatonic Harmony, and Further Extensions of the Phrase Model

EXERCISE 15.1   Bass Line Dictation

 Notate bass lines of the short progressions that contain the submediant harmony; provide roman numerals. Since this exercise continues to develop tonal memory, begin by listening and memorizing before notating pitches. Focus on the deeper-level harmonic functions. For example, since a tonic prolongation will most likely begin the exercise, ask yourself how long tonic is prolonged before it yields to a new harmonic function. Do not focus on details (such as the type of contrapuntal chords used to expand the tonic) until the last hearing, during which you are encouraged to refine your answer. Always begin with the large picture, which should include questions such as "How long is the excerpt?" "Is it a progression, a prolongation, or both?" "Where does the tonic prolongation end?" and so on.

A.

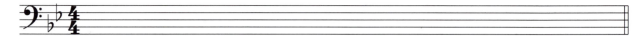

B.

C.

D.

E.

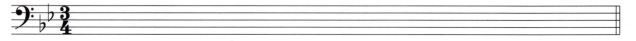

EXERCISE 15.2 Outer-Voice Dictation

You now notate bass and soprano voices of progressions that include the submediant harmony. A few pitches are provided. Analyze using two levels.

E.

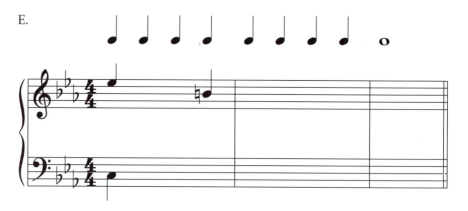

EXERCISE 15.3 Dictation of Figurated Excerpts Using the Submediant

 Notate the bass of each example that contains one or two statements of the submediant. Provide roman numerals, and label the harmonic function for each statement of the submediant.

A.

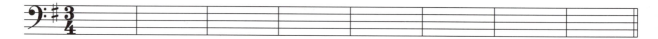

B.

C.

EXERCISE 15.4 Figured Bass

Write a soprano part for the figured bass and add the inner voices. Provide a two-level analysis.

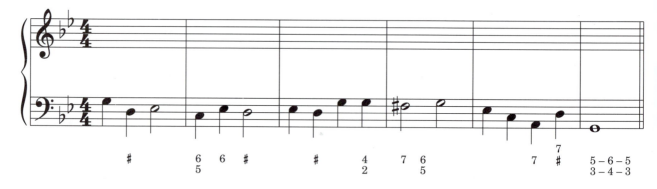

EXERCISE 15.5   Analysis and Dictation

The bass lines are omitted from the literature excerpts below. Based on listening and with the assistance of the upper voices, notate the missing voice and add roman numerals.

A.   Schubert, Impromptu in G♭ major, op. 90, D. 899

B.   Haydn, *Andante*, Symphony No. 104 in D major, "London," Hob. I. 102

C.   Haydn, *Adagio*, String Quartet in E♭ major ("Fantasia"), op. 76, no. 6, Hob. III. 80

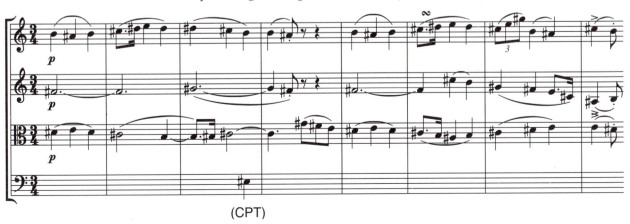

(CPT)

D.   Mascagni, "O Lola," *Cavalleria Rusticana* ("Rustic Chivalry"), scene i

. . . porta;
Se per te mojo e vado in paradiso,

Non c'entro se non vedo il tuo
     bel viso

. . . ever;
Yet would I seek your love, though it
     destroy me,
Suffer the pain and sorrow if you
     were near me!

EXAMPLE 15.6   Illustrations

Complete the tasks below in four voices and analyze.

A.   In any minor key, write a progression that includes the following (tasks appear in order of composition):

1.   a tonic prolongation that includes one suspension figure
2.   a descending bass arpeggiation that includes the submediant
3.   a pre-dominant that is expanded by voice exchange
4.   a dominant that includes one suspension figure

B.   In any major key (except C), write a progression that includes the following tasks. Begin by logically ordering the tasks so that your progression makes harmonic sense.

1.   a deceptive harmonic progression
2.   a bass suspension
3.   a tonic expansion using a passing figure in the bass
4.   a nondominant seventh chord
5.   a descending fifth progression using vi

EXERCISE 15.7   Analysis

Below are three different harmonizations by Bach of the opening of the chorale tune "Jesu meine Freude" from his *St. Matthew Passion*. Analyze each setting carefully, then write a paragraph comparing and contrasting the settings. Which do you like best and why?

A.

B.

C.

Weg mit al - len Schit - zen!
Weg ihr eit - len Eh - ren,

Weg, weg mit al - len Schit - zen
Weg, weg ihr eit - len Eh - - ren

Weg, weg, weg, weg mit al-len Schit - - zen
Web, weg, weg, weg ihr eit-len Eh - - ren

Weg, weg, weg, weg mit al-len Schit - zen
Weg, weg, weg, weg ihr eit-len Eh - ren

EXERCISE 15.8 Harmonizing Melodic Fragments Using the Submediant

Choose an appropriate meter and rhythmic setting. Then, harmonize the soprano fragments below by using at least one submediant harmony in each example; analyze.

A.

B.

C.

EXERCISE 15.9 Step-Descent Bass Analysis

Listen to each excerpt, determining first whether there is a direct, tetrachordal descent to V, or whether there is an indirect descent of a fifth. Finally, analyze using two levels.

A. Handel, "Thou Art Gone Up," *Messiah*, HWV 56

Is there a textual motivation for the contour of the vocal line? What effect does this contour create with the bass?

Thou art   gone up on high,   Thou   art gone up   on high

B. Handel, Sarabande, Suite in G minor, HWV 253
In this example the descent occurs on the downbeat chords. The intervening weak-beat chords elaborate it. The elaboration may be viewed as essential, given the voice-leading problems that would result if they were absent.

C.   Corelli, *Vivace*, Concerto Grosso No. 8 in G minor, op. 6

D.   Grieg, "Folkevise" ("Folksong"), *Lyriske stykker II (Lyric Pieces II)*, op. 38, no. 2
Consider the recurring bass pitch, B^1, to be a pedal.

EXERCISE 15.10   Dictation

Notate the bass and soprano and provide roman numerals. Label the function for each occurrence of the submediant harmony. Your choices are: descending root arpeggiation, circle of fifths, deceptive motion, pre-dominant (VI moves directly to V), and mixture of harmonic and contrapuntal: the step-descent bass.

EXERCISE 15.11   Dictation from the Literature

 Notate the bass and provide roman numerals. You need not notate repeated pitches.

A. Bach, "Alles ist an Gottes Segen," BWV 263

Andante

IV   VII⁶ III

B. Bach, "Ermutre dich, mein schwacher Geist," *Christmas Oratorio*, no. 12, BWV 248

Andante

C. Carissimi, "Plorate filii Israel," *Jeptha*

Andante

D. Schubert, "Am Bach im Frühling" ("To the Brook in Springtime"), D. 361

Andante

(use triplets)

E. Grieg, "Melodie," op. 47

EXERCISE 15.12   Writing the Step-Descent Bass

Realize in four voices the figured basses below that contain step-descent basses. Include a two-level analysis.

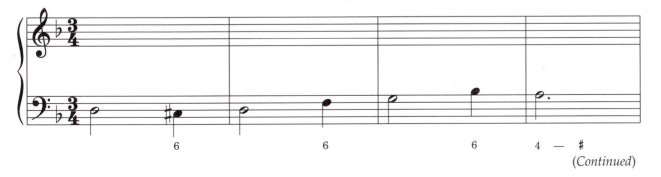

6   6   6

4 — ♯

(Continued)

(Continued)

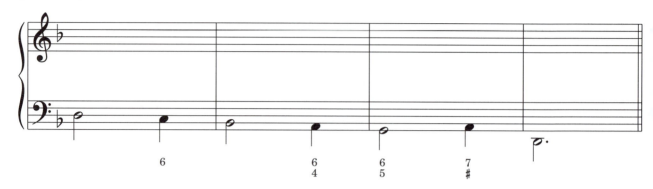

EXERCISE 15.13　Keyboard: Step-Descent Basses

Realize the contrapuntal models below in four voices. Be able to sing either outer voice while playing the other three. Transpose each model to C and B minor.

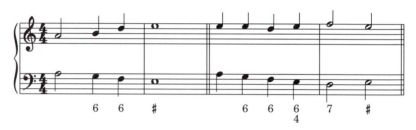

EXERCISE 15.14　Keyboard: Figured Bass

Create a good soprano line and add inner voices; you may write out the soprano. Analyze, and be able to sing the bass while playing the other three voices.

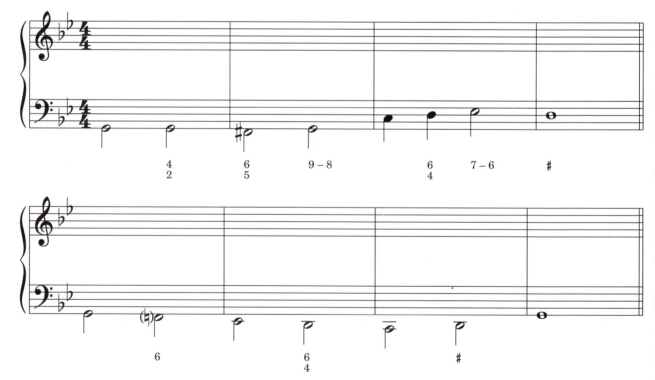

EXERCISE 15.15   Keyboard: Figuration

You will now create a figurated piece from the figured bass you realized in Exercise 15.14. Below is one realization of mm. 1–2 of Example 15.14, followed by common figurations used in Baroque keyboard music. Choose one that you like or develop your own, then play Exercise 15.14 in the figurated style.

EXERCISE 15.16   Keyboard: Harmonizing the Ascending Scale

We know that by combining two or more harmonic cells, we can create longer progressions. One such progression is a complete stepwise octave ascent. We will learn one harmonization for the ascending soprano and one for the ascending bass. Study the figures and realize in four voices. Individual harmonic cells are marked with brackets. Be able to sing either outer voice while playing the other three voices. Play in major and minor keys up to and including three sharps and three flats ($\hat{6}$ will be raised in minor, as noted).

soprano scale   bass scale

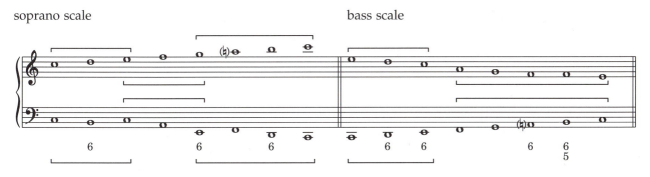

EXERCISE 15.17   Keyboard: Illustrations

Complete one of the two illustrations below in your choice of meter (tasks need not appear in the order given). Hint: Study each carefully, for it might be possible to save time by combining one or more tasks (e.g., the following four individual tasks can be made into a single contrapuntal expansion of tonic: a suspension, an ECM, a bass arpeggiation, and a P$_4^6$ chord).

In D minor:

A. VI in a bass arpeggiation
B. a direct step-descent bass V
C. at least two suspensions
D. a contrapuntal expansion using ii_2^4
E. a ii_5^6 in the final half cadence

In B minor:

A. a lament bass that descends to $\hat{4}$
B. a $_4^6$ chord
C. at least one suspension
D. a deceptive progression
E. a iv7 in the final cadence

The Mediant, the Back-Relating Dominant, and a Synthesis of Diatonic Harmonic Relationships

EXERCISE 16.1   Dictation

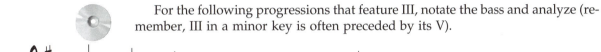

For the following progressions that feature III, notate the bass and analyze (remember, III in a minor key is often preceded by its V).

A.

B.

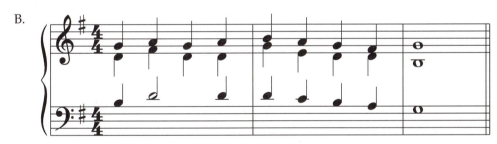

C.

D.

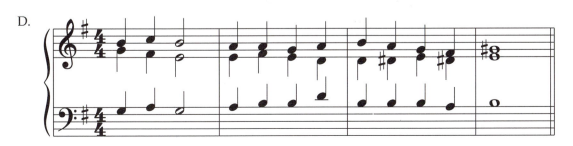

E.   Wagner, "Bridal Chorus," *Lohengrin,* act 3, scene 1

Treulich gefürht Ziehet dahin,   Faithfully led, enter this place,
Wo euch der Segen der Lieve   Where there await you the blessings of
  bewah'r!   Love
Siegfreicher Muth, Minnegewinn,   Valorous might, radiant grace
Eint euch in Treue zum selifsten Paar Here are united by heaven above.

F.   Beethoven, *Andante,* Piano Sonata No. 25 in G major, op. 79

G.   Schubert, Impromptu in A♭ major, op. 90, D. 899, no. 4

EXERCISE 16.2   Figured Bass

The following figured bass examples include III and VI. Write a soprano voice, provide a first- and second-level analysis, and then add the inner voices.

A.

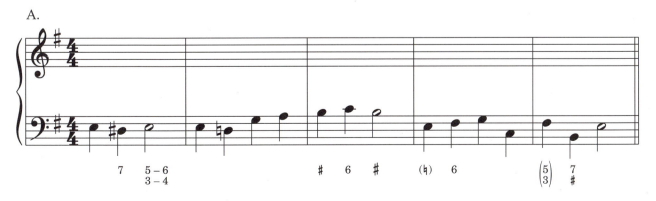

B.

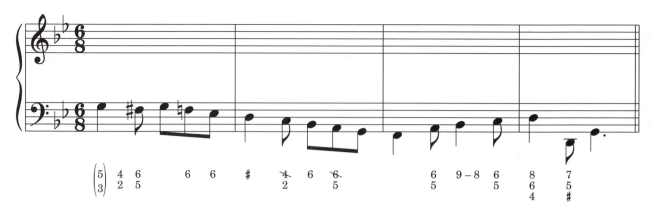

EXERCISE 16.3   Analysis and Dictation

 Analyze the following examples with two-level analysis. All of the examples are missing some or all of their bass lines; notate them.

A.   Mozart, *Menuetto,* Symphony No. 35 in D major, K. 385

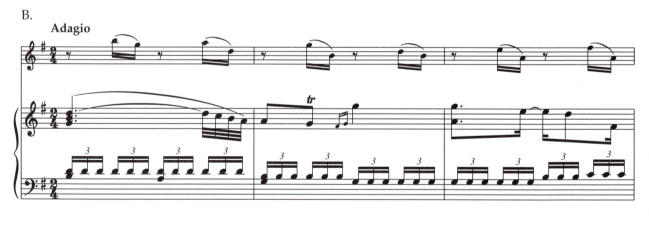

B.   Mozart, *Adagio,* Violin Sonata in D major, K. 7 (written at the age of seven)

B.

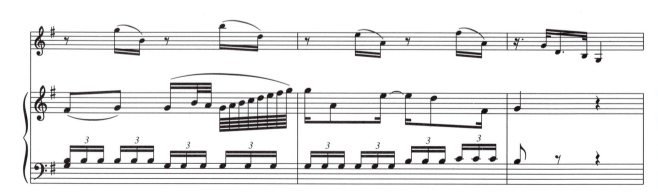

C. Brahms, "Da unten im Tale" ("Down in the Valley There"), *Deutsche Volkslieder*, WoO. 33, no. 6

1. Da unten im Tale Läufts Wasser so trüb, Und i kann dirs net sagen, I hab' di so lieb.	Down in the valley there the water flows so sadly, and I can't tell you that I love you so.
2. Sprichst allweil von Lieb', Sprichst allewil von Treu', Und a bissele Falschheit Is auch wohl dabei!	You always speak of love, you always speak of fidelity, but a bit of falsehood is always there too!

D. Schubert, "Ave Maria," D. 839

D.

$(vii^{ø6}_6/V)$
5

E. Handel, "I Know That My Redeemer Liveth," *Messiah*, HWV 56

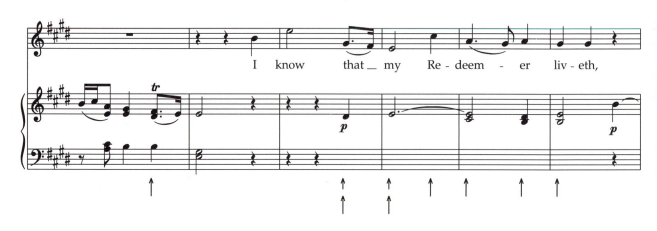

I know   that _ my   Re - deem - er   liv - eth,

F. Tchaikovsky, "June," *The Seasons*, op. 37b, no. 6

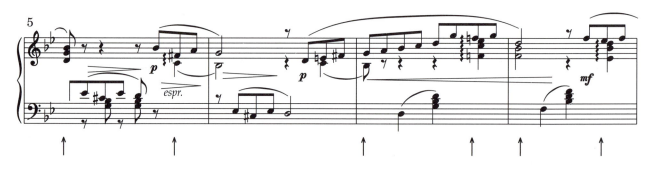

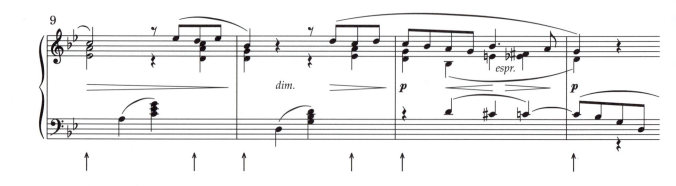

G.   Rossini, "Una voce poco fa," *Il barbiere di Siviglia (The Barber of Seville)*, act I, scene 9.

... [Il mio] cor ferito è già,   ... [He that] sang was young and cheerful.
E Lindor fu che il piagò.   And Lindoro, that was his name.
Sì, Lindoro mio sarà!   Yes, Lindoro shall be mine!
Lo giurai, la vincerò.   Yes, I swear it, I shall win the game.

H.   Haydn, "Es vollbracht," *The Seven Last Words*, op. 51, no. 6, Hob. III. 55

EXERCISE 16.4   Multiple Harmonization of a Soprano Melody

Harmonize each of the melodies below in at least three significantly different ways (in four voices). Include at least one example of the mediant and the submediant harmonies in each harmonization. Determine the mode; it is often possible to cast

the tune in both a major key and its relative minor. Review the process of harmonizing a melody that was presented at the end of Chapter 14. Play each solution on the piano, singing either outer voice while playing the other three voices.

A.

B.

EXERCISE 16.5   Keyboard: Multiple Harmonizations

Harmonize the melodic fragment below in three different ways. Include at least
one statement of vi or iii in each harmonization. You may wish to set this melody
in major and its relative minor.

EXERCISE 16.6   Dictation

The following six exercises contain the upper voices of progressions that include
various functions of III and VI. Notate the bass and choose one example to do a
two-level analysis. Begin by bracketing short, complete progressions. For example, a tonic expansion may be followed by a cadential area with deceptive motion, and so forth. There may be more than a single motion to the cadence. Study
the chord progression and its interpretation below.

I vii°6 I6	ii6 V vi	IV vii°6 I iii	IV V I
I expanded	Deceptive cadence	return to tonic with contrapuntal cadence	bass arpeggiation through mediant to PAC

A.

B.

C.

D.

E.

F.

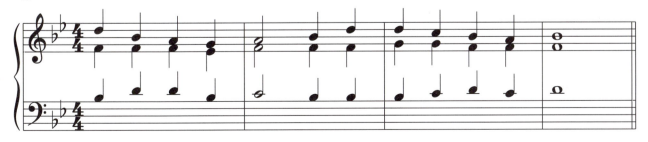

EXERCISE 16.7   Analysis: Back-Relating Dominants

Below are examples in which the dominant prominently appears. Determine whether the dominant is structural (that is, it moves the harmonic progression forward) or whether it is a voice-leading chord (e.g., a passing chord in a bass descent to vi or a weak back-relating dominant).

A.

B.

C.

D.   Mozart, *Allegro,* Piano Sonata in D major, K. 576

(vii$^{\circ}_6$/ii)

E.   Beethoven, *Menuetto: Allegro*, Piano Sonata No. 7 in D major, op. 10, no. 3

(V_3^4/ii)

F.   Schubert, Frühlings

EXERCISE 16.8 Keyboard: Figured Bass and Back-Relating Dominants

Realize the figured bass below. Explain the function of each dominant harmony.

EXERCISE 16.9 Dictation

Notate the outer voices of the homophonic examples below that contain BRDs. Provide a first- and second-level analysis. A few notes are given.

A.

B.

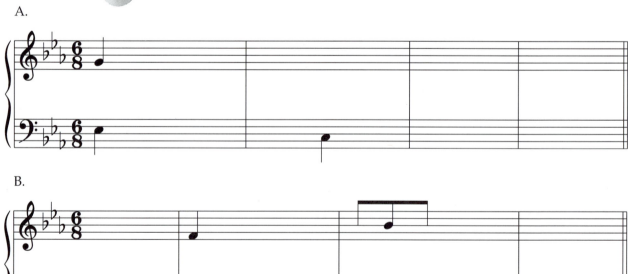

C.

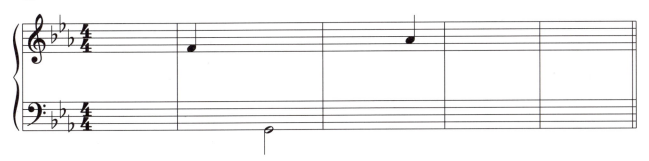

D.

E.

EXERCISE 16.10   Dictation

 Listen to the figurated exercises for flute with piano accompaniment. Notate the bass line of the piano and provide a roman numeral analysis.

A.

B.

EXERCISE 16.11   Soprano and Bass Figures

Based on harmonic patterns that you've learned and the implications of the figures and soprano line, add a bass line, roman numerals, and the inner voices. The absence of figures implies root position and ties indicate a stationary bass. Include one example of vi and iii in each exercise.

A.

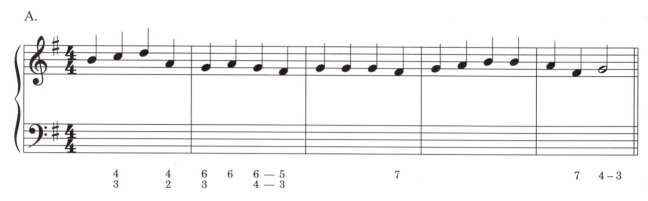

B.

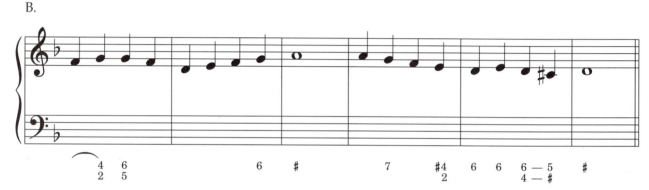

EXERCISE 16.12 Keyboard: Expansions of a Harmonic Model

The following harmonic models present a standard tonic–pre-dominant–dominant–tonic progression. Choose an appropriate meter and expand each stage as required by the instructions. Analyze your work.

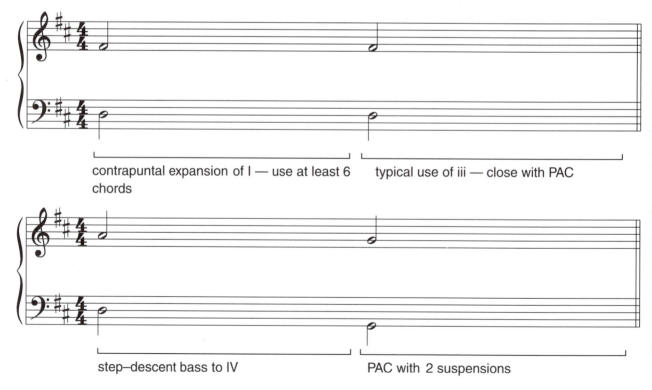

contrapuntal expansion of I — use at least 6 chords   typical use of iii — close with PAC

step–descent bass to IV   PAC with 2 suspensions

EXERCISE 16.13   Keyboard: Continuation of Figurated Textures

Play the first half of the exercise as written. Complete the exercise by realizing the figured bass and continuing the pattern of figuration. Add appropriate tones of figuration.

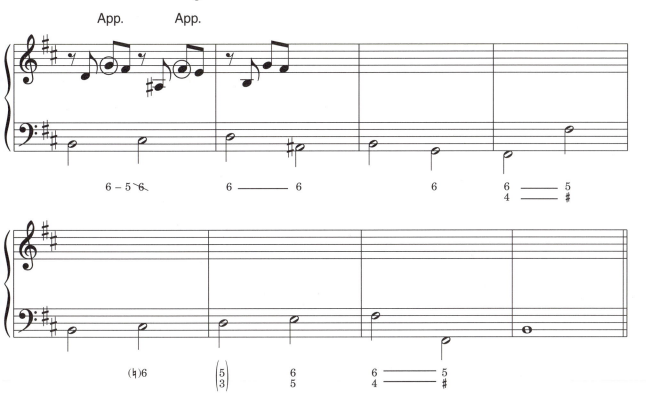

EXERCISE 16.14   Analytical Synthesis

Below are three pairs of excerpts. The members of each pair share musical characteristics, such as harmonic progression. There are, of course, contrasting features as well. Listen to and analyze each pair; then, in a paragraph, compare and contrast the examples.

A1.   Mozart, Piano Sonata in A minor, K. 310

A2.   Mozart, *Andante cantabile,* Piano Sonata in C major, K. 330

B1.   Schumann, "Arabesque," op. 18

B2.   Schumann, "Kind im Einschlummern" *Kinderszenen ("Scenes from Child-hood"),* op. 15, no. 12

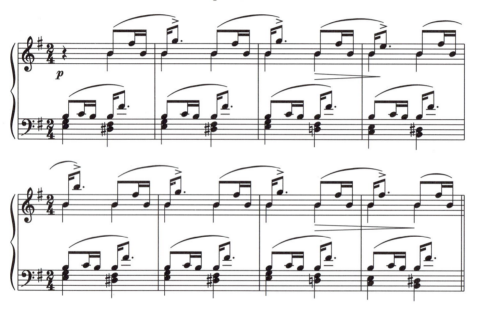

C1.   Grieg, "Norwegian Dance," op. 47
The A♯ that appears in mm. 7 to 10 is the temporary leading tone of the harmony that controls these measures. A single harmony is extended in mm. 11 to 16.

C2. Mahler, "Die zwei blauen Augen" ("The Two Blue Eyes"), *Lieder eines fahren-den Gesellen (Songs of a Wayfarer)*, no. 4

Die zwei blauen Augen von meinem Schatz,	The two blue eyes of my beloved—
Die haben mich in die weite Welt geschickt.	they have sent me into the wide world.
Da musst ich Abschied nehmen	I had to take my leave
Vom allerliebsten Platz! . . .	of this most charming place! . . .

EXERCISE 16.15   Unfigured Bass and Soprano

Determine cadences and implied harmonies using roman numerals. Expect to encounter step descents, the mediant and submediant, and BRDs. Add inner voices and a second-level analysis. Then, add tones of figuration to create a more fluid sound, distributing them between voices in order to create a balanced texture.

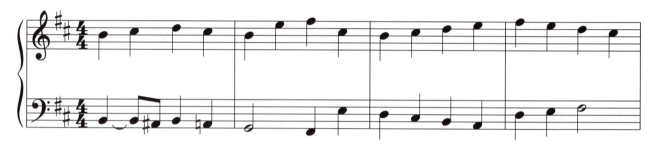

EXERCISE 16.16   Unfigured Bass

Label cadences and locate harmonic cells; add roman numerals. Label remaining harmonies, then add a soprano melody and inner voices.

EXERCISE 16.17   Small Compositional Projects

Complete the following tasks in four voices.

A. Choose an appropriate meter and harmonize the soprano scale degrees $\hat{3}$–$\hat{3}$–$\hat{2}$–$\hat{1}$–$\hat{7}$–$\hat{2}$–$\hat{1}$–$\hat{7}$–$\hat{6}$–$\hat{5}$ in D major and G minor in two different ways.

B. In the key of C minor, write a four-measure phrase using a mixture of half and quarter notes in the soprano, each of which is harmonized, that contains the following:

1. a deceptive progression
2. three different types of $^6_4$ chords
3. a voice exchange
4. two suspensions, one of which occurs in the bass

C. In B minor, write an eight-measure composition comprising two four-measure phrases that contain the following:

1. a descending bass tetrachord
2. a typical use of the mediant
3. a half cadence
4. a phrygian cadence

EXERCISE 16.18   Keyboard: Descending Scale Harmonization

We now harmonize descending soprano scales (ascending scales were presented in Chapter 15). Study each model and realize according to the figured bass. Note that the mediant appears in setting the descending line $\hat{8}$–$\hat{7}$. Be able to sing either outer-part scale while playing the other voices. Transpose each to another key of your choice.

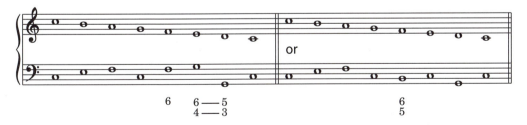

EXERCISE 16.19   Keyboard: Figured Bass and Singing from the Literature

Sing the tunes that follow and determine their key. Then, realize the figured bass in four voices and analyze. Finally, combine singing and realizing the figured bass at the keyboard.

A. Handel, "What Do I Hear," *Saul,* act I, scene 3, HWV 53

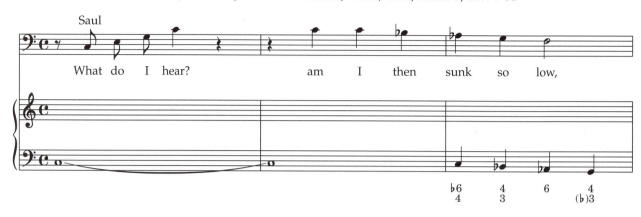

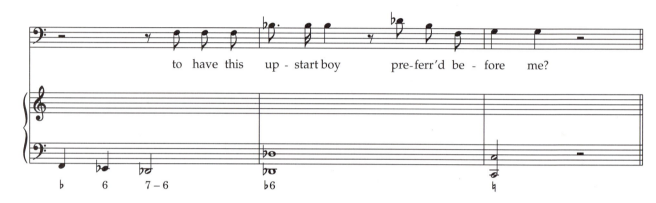

B. Stradella, "Pietà, Signore!" ("Have Pity, Lord"), S11–27 (by Fétis)

. . . se a te giunge il mio pregar;   . . . if my prayer rises to you:
non mi punisca   do not chastise me
il tuo rigor.   in your severity.

C. Torelli, "Tu lo sai"

Io non bra - mo al - tra mer - cè   Ma ri
Oth - er plea - sure I do not crave   Than thou

cor - da - ti di me,   E poi sprez - za un _ in - fe - del,
think - est _ once on me,   Then for - tet - test me _ and all my pain,

EXERCISE 16.20   Variation and Expansion

Each of the models below is followed by a series of variations and expansions that flesh out each model's basic progression. Notate the outer voices and analyze each of the expansions.

Model A

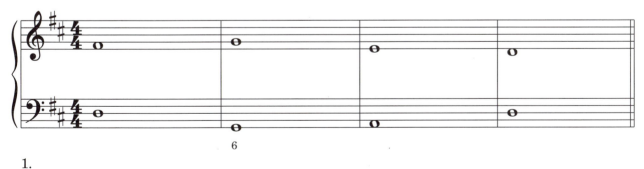

6

1.

2.

3.

4.

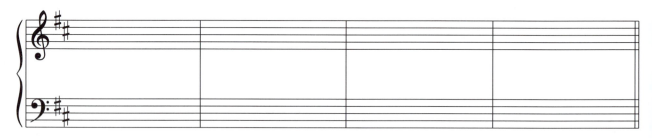

5.

Model B

1.

2.

3.

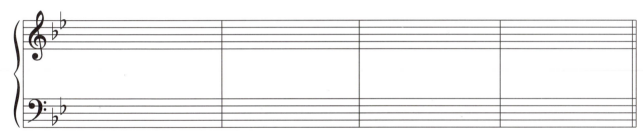

4.

5.

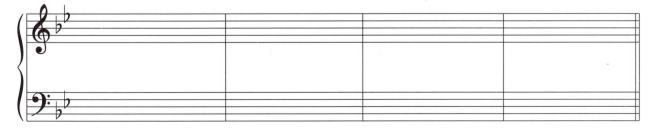

CHAPTER 17

The Period

EXERCISE 17.1   Cadential Warm-up (Review)

We now briefly review cadences. Label each cadence in the excerpts below. Your choices are: perfect authentic (PAC); imperfect authentic (IAC); half (HC); phrygian (PHRY); and deceptive (DC, the deceptive cadence, as we learned, is more accurately described as a "deceptive progression" given that most deceptive progressions create subphrases, and do not close phrases. Rather, the phrase will continue to the PD and D functions); and plagal (PC; more accurately described as "plagal motion," since most follow an authentic cadence and therefore function to extend the tonic). Be aware that authentic cadences are of two types: perfect cadences are those that have strong harmonic and melodic motions. Imperfect cadences include not only melodic closure on $\hat{3}$ or $\hat{5}$, but the label also extends to contrapuntal cadences, which contain inverted dominant (or dominant function) harmonies or inverted tonic harmonies.

A.   Haydn, *Adagio,* String Quartet in F minor, op. 20, no. 5, Hob. III. 35

B.   Rossini, "L'amoroso e sincero Lindoro," ("Your Loving and Sincere Lindoro"),
Il barbiere di Siviglia (*The Barber of Seville*), act I, scene 6

L'amoroso e sincero Lindoro,
non può darvi, mia cara, un tesoro. . . .

Your loving and sincere Lindoro,
Cannot put before you, my dear, a
treasure. . . .

C.   Beethoven, *Allegretto*, Piano Sonata No. 9 in E major, op. 14, no. 1

D.   Bach, *Larghetto*, Concerto for Oboe d'Amore in A major, BWV 1055
There may be more than one cadence.

(*Continued*)

(*Continued*)

E.   Bach, Prelude in B♭ major, *Well-Tempered Clavier*, Book 1, BWV 866

EXERCISE 17.2 Phrase and Subphrase Identification

Label phrases and subphrases using brackets. Label cadences as in Exercise 17.1.

A. Mendelssohn, *Lieder ohne Worte* ("Songs without Words"), Book 5, No. 6 in A major, op. 62

B. Haydn, *Moderato*, Piano Sonata No. 35 in A♭ major, Hob. XVI. 34

C. Chopin, Waltz in E minor, BI 56

EXERCISE 17.3 Analysis of Periods

Make period diagrams of each example below and include a label and any comments that support your interpretation or illuminate motivic structures. Note: Some examples are not periods.

A. Mozart, *Allegro assai*, String Quartet No. 19 in C major, "Dissonant," K. 465

B. Chopin, Mazurka in D major, op. 33, no. 2, BI 115

C. Wagner, Pilgrim's Chorus, *Tannhauser*, act. 3

D. Beethoven, *Adagio cantabile*, Romance in F major for Violin and Orchestra, op. 50

E. Lehar, Waltz, from *The Merry Widow*

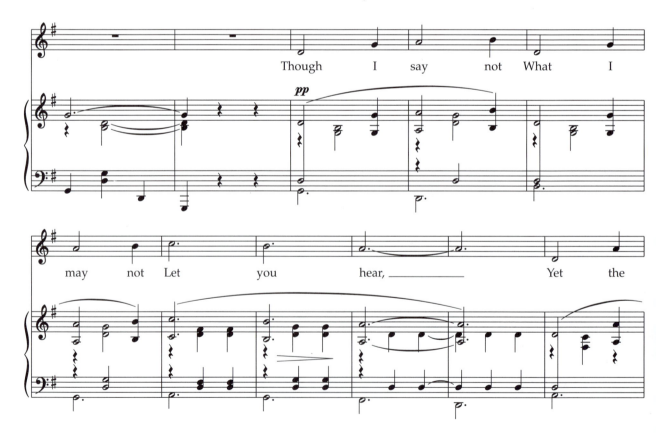

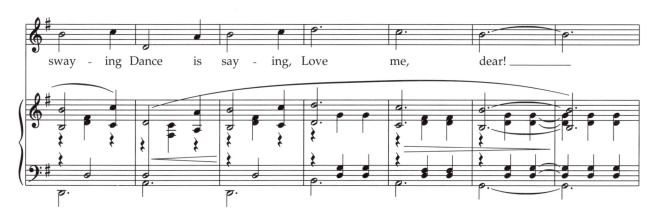

sway - ing Dance   is   say - ing, Love   me,   dear!

F. Beethoven, *Scherzo: Allegretto,* Piano Sonata No. 2 in A major, op. 2, no. 2
The chord in measure 3 functions as a local dominant of the dominant. We take
up such "applied chords" in Chapter 21.

G. Mozart, *Andante cantabile,* Piano Sonata in C major, K. 330
Be aware of subphrases.

EXERCISE 17.4   Period Structures and Dictation

For this exercise, notate missing soprano and/or bass voices (arrows indicate missing pitches), and provide a roman numeral analysis and period diagram.

A. Beethoven, *Adagio,* Piano Sonata No. 1 in F minor, op. 2, no. 1

B. Schubert, "Frühlingstraum" ("A Dream of Springtime"), *Winterreise,* D. 911, no. 11

What is unusual about the phrase lengths?

1. Ich träum-te von bun - ten Blu - men,   so wie sie wohl blü - hen im Mai,   ich
2. Ich träum-te von Lieb   im Lie - be,   von ei – ner schö - nonMaid,   von

träum-te von grü-non Wie - sen, von lu-sti gem-Vo-gel-ge - schrei, _ von _ lu-sti gem-Vo-gel ge-schrei.
Her - zen und von Küs - sen, vonWonne-und Se - lig-keit,_ von_ won-ne und Se - leg-keit.

Ich träumte von bunten Blumen,   I dreamed of colorful flowers
So wie sie wohl blühen im Mai;   Just as bloom in May;
Ich träumte von grünen Wiesen,   I dreamed of green meadows,
Von lustigem Vogelgeschrei.   Of merry bird songs.

Ich träumte von Lieb' um Liebe, I dreamed of love because of love,
Von einer schönen Maid,   Of a beautiful girl,
Von Herzen und von Küssen,   Of hearts and of kisses,
Von Wonne und Seligkeit.   Of bliss and happiness.

C. Mozart, *Allegretto,* Trio for Piano, Clarinet, and Viola in E♭ major, K. 498

D. Beethoven, *Marcia funebre: Adagio assai,* Symphony No. 3 in E♭ major, "Eroica," op. 55

E.   Mozart Concerto for Horn in E♭, K. 447, "Romance"

EXERCISE 17.5   Sing and Play: Improvising Period Structures

Below are two antecedent phrases that lack a consequent. Sing and play these phrases (if you have trouble with the accompaniments as given, you may play block chords in the right hand). Now, improvise/work out a consequent phrase that closes on the tonic in order to create a period. Your first step will be to determine the period type you want. After designing the tonal plan and cadence of the second phrase, improvise both a parallel and a contrasting consequent. Be prepared to perform your periods in class.

A.   Beethoven, "Ich liebe dich" ("I Love You"), WoO 132

Ich liebe dich, so wie du mich,   I love you as you love me,
Am Abend und am Morgen,   in the evening and the morning,

B.   Mendelssohn, "Wenn sich zwei Herzen Scheiden" ("When Two Hearts Separate"), op. 99, no. 5

1. Wenn sich zwei Her - zen schei - den, die sich der - einst ge - liebt,

Wenn sich zwei Herzen scheiden,   When two hearts separate themselves from
Die sich dereinst geliebt,   who each other once loved

EXERCISE 17.6   Completing Figurated Periods

Maintaining the texture and the harmonic rhythm of mm. 1–4, write a consequent phrase that complements each given antecedent phrase. Provide a full label for the period.

A.

B.

EXERCISE 17.7   Figured Bass

The following figured basses are presented in an unmetered context. First, determine roman numerals and possible cadences for each. Then, attempt to fit each into a periodic structure by imposing a meter and providing each note with the proper duration. Make sure that there is no more than one chord per quarter note in $\frac{3}{4}$ or $\frac{4}{4}$ or one chord per eighth note in $\frac{6}{8}$.

A.

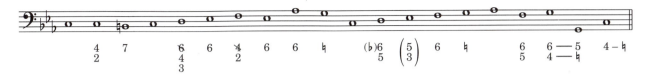

$$\begin{matrix} 4 \\ 2 \end{matrix} \quad 7 \qquad \begin{matrix} 6 \\ 4 \\ 3 \end{matrix} \quad 6 \quad \begin{matrix} 4 \\ 2 \end{matrix} \quad 6 \quad 6 \quad \natural \qquad (\flat)6 \atop 5 \quad \left(\begin{matrix} 5 \\ 3 \end{matrix}\right) \quad 6 \quad \natural \qquad \begin{matrix} 6 \\ 5 \end{matrix} \quad \begin{matrix} 6 - 5 \\ 4 - \natural \end{matrix} \quad 4 - \natural$$

B.

$$6 \quad 7 \qquad \begin{matrix} 4 \\ 2 \end{matrix} \quad 6 \quad 6 \qquad \begin{matrix} 4 \\ 2 \end{matrix} \quad 6 \quad 6 \qquad \left(\begin{matrix} 5 \\ 3 \end{matrix}\right) \quad \begin{matrix} 5 - 6 \\ 5 \end{matrix} \quad 8 - 7 \quad \begin{matrix} 5\text{-}6\text{-}3 \\ 3\text{-}4\text{-}3 \end{matrix}$$

EXERCISE 17.8   Writing Homophonic Periods

Write two different homophonic (SATB) periods. Cast one in major, the other in minor, and use one duple and one triple meter. Each should be eight measures, with each measure containing at least one but not more than two harmonies. Add tones of figuration to your upper voice. Analyze the period type and the harmonies.

EXERCISE 17.9   Writing Florid Periods

Write two different periods, both of which contain a florid melody that is accompanied by three- or four-voice harmonies. You might approach this exercise in one of two ways. In the first scenario, you would conceive of the work with the harmonic aspect at the forefront of your compositional process. Thus, you would compose for a wind or string trio, voicing individual harmonies for the specific instruments. Once the harmonic underpinning is complete, you would then add a florid tune above for a solo instrument. In the second scenario, you would first write your soloist's tune and then add the harmonic underpinning beneath in the form of the three-voice accompaniment. If you employ this second technique, you must constantly consider implied harmonies in your soloist's line, perhaps using roman numerals to remind you of which chords to use when you return to the harmonic underpinning. Your accompaniment may be strictly homophonic, or more figurated, with simple arpeggiations or broken chords derived from offsetting the vertical voices that you have previously written. You could score this for the right hand of the piano, then add a left-hand part that moves more slowly in octaves and which carries the harmony.

EXERCISE 17.10   Variation and Contrapuntal Expansion of a Harmonic Model

You will hear contrapuntal expansions of two I–V–I harmonic progressions and one period. Each of the three model bass lines below will be fleshed out in variations that maintain the metric placement of the given harmonies implied by the bass notes. Complete the following tasks:

1. Notate the bass and soprano voices of the contrapuntal chords that embellish the given harmonic structure.
2. Provide a two-level harmonic analysis. Your harmonic vocabulary now in-

cludes: I, I6, IV6, V, V6, V7, V^6_5, V^4_3, V^4_2, vii°6, vii°7, vii°$^6_5$, and vii°$^4_3$, the predominants: ii, ii6, ii7, ii$^6_5$, ii$^4_3$, IV, IV6, IV7, IV$^6_5$, and the new harmonies: vi and iii (and VII in minor).

Model A (single phrase)

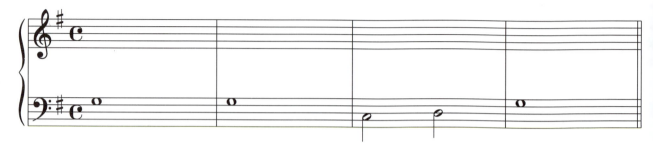

1.

2.

3.

4.

Model B (single phrase)

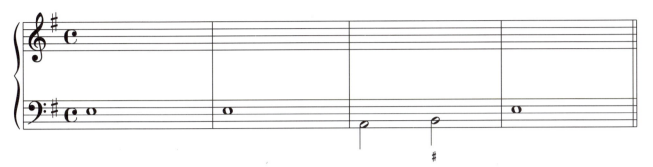

1.

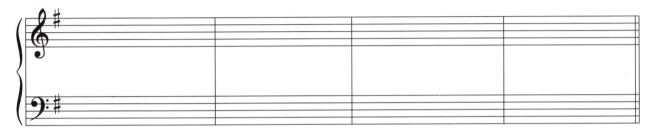

2.

3.

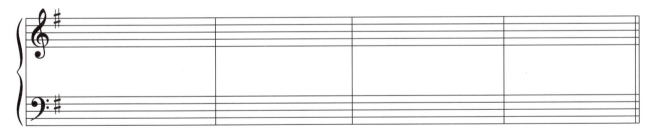

Model C (Beware: Two of the variations do not strictly follow the model.)

1.

2.

3.

4.

5.

6.

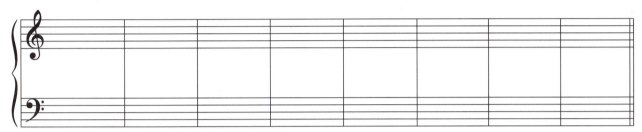

7.

EXERCISE 17.11   Folk Tunes and Periodic Structure

We now harmonize tunes taken from traditional American songs, Christmas carols, and other familiar sources. All examples contain more than a single phrase, but not every example forms a period; some are simply repeated phrases. Choose three or four tunes from the list below whose first two phrases combine into one of the three period types that we are currently writing (we will postpone writing progressive periods until Chapter 22). Then, write out the tune from memory, making sure that you use a suitable meter. Next, determine the type of period and add the bass line at the cadences and include roman numerals. Then, harmonize the tune using an appropriate harmonic rhythm; that is, not every note of the tune will be harmonized. You will need to determine the tones of figuration. Add a bass line and inner voices. Use only harmonies that we have studied.

"Home on the Range"
"Shall We Gather at the River"
"Swing Low, Sweet Chariot"
"Amazing Grace"
"Pop Goes the Weasel"
"Beautiful Dreamer"
"The Cowboy's Lament (The Streets of Laredo)"
"Deck the Halls"
"God Rest Ye Merry, Gentlemen"
"Good King Wenceslas"
"It Came Upon the Midnight Clear"
"Jingle Bells" (refrain)
"Auld Lang Syne"
"Old Folks at Home (Way Down Upon the Suwannee River)"
"Clementine"
"I've Been Workin' on the Railroad"

CHAPTER 18

Other Small Musical Structures: Sentences, Double Periods, and Asymmetrical Periods

EXERCISE 18.1   Melody Harmonization: The Sentence

The melodies below are cast in sentence structure. They may take the form of single four-measure phrases or eight-measure periods comprising two four-measure phrases. Determine cadential points and add appropriate bass notes. Then, harmonize the rest of the tune. Remember, the two subphrases that together make up half of the sentence should be related, though they need not have identical harmonizations.

EXERCISE 18.2   Writing Sentence Structures

Write an eight-measure period that is cast in sentence structure (2 + 2 + 4 measures). Begin either by improvising on your own instrument, by singing, or by sitting at the piano in order to find a suitable melodic and rhythmic motive in a meter, key, and mode of your choice. The first part of your sentence will be a two-measure unit that will be repeated either literally, or with small changes, to make up four measures. The second part of your sentence will be a single four-measure idea that should borrow at least some elements from the opening two-measure idea. As you write your tunes, consider the underlying harmonic structure and its harmonic rhythm; you may even wish to sketch in a few bass notes and roman numerals. The harmonic structure should approximate the model below.

A (2 mm.)   A' (2 mm.)   B (4 mm.)
I——I or V   I——I or V   I———PAC

EXERCISE 18.3   Melody Harmonization and Period Structure

Determine the type of period and whether it is cast in sentence structure. Choose two examples and determine their harmonic rhythm; then, harmonize implied cadences and the rest of the tune. Provide formal labels, roman numerals, and figured bass.

A.   Mozart, *Rondeau: Tempo di Menuetto*, Bassoon Concerto in B♭ major, K. 191

B.   Schubert, "Wiegenlied" ("Cradle Song"), op. 92, no. 2, D. 498

Langsam (Lento)

Schla - fe, schla - fe, hol - der, sü - sser Kna - be, lei - se wiegt dich dei - ner Mut - ter Hand;

Schlafe, holder, süsser Knabe,
Leise wiegt dich deiner Mutter Hand; . . .

C.   Mozart, *Allegro*, Horn Concerto in D major, K. 412

D.   Schubert, "An mein Klavier" ("To My Clavier"), D. 342

Mässig (Moderato)

1. Sanf - tes Kla - vier,   sanf - tes Kla - vier!   wel - che Ent - zük - kun - gen schaf - fest du mir!
2. Bin   ich al - lein,   bin   ich al - lein,   hauch' ich dir mei - ne Emp - fin - dungen ein,
3. Sing ich da - zu,   sing ich da - zu,   gol - de - ner Flü - gel, welch himm - li - sche Ruh
4. Sanf - tes Kla - vier,   sanf - tes Kla - vier!   wel - che Ent - zük - kun - gen schaf - test du mir!

1. Sanftes Klavier,   Soft-toned clavier,
   Welche Entzückungen   What charms
   Schaffest du mir, . . .   You create for me . . .

2. Bin ich allein,   When I am alone,
   Hauch' ich dir meine   I breathe my
   Empfindungen ein, . . .   thoughts to you. . . .

3. Sing' ich dazu,   If I sing as I play
   Goldener Flügel,   Golden instrument,
   welch' himmlische Ruh' . . .   What heavenly peace . . .

4. Sanftes Klavier,   Soft-toned clavier,
   Welche Entzückungen   What charms
   schaffest du mir, . . .   You create for me . . .

E. Mozart, *Allegro,* Horn Concerto in D major, K. 412

EXERCISE 18.4   Harmonic Models and Periods and Sentences

Choose two of the following harmonic models to write periods or double periods. Some examples work well as sentences. Decide on a key, meter, and harmonic rhythm, and add a bass voice. Finally, add a tune for voice or solo instrument and complete the texture by adding the missing chord tones to the implied harmonies above your bass, the result of which will be a homophonic accompaniment to your melody.

PHRASE 1:

A. I–extended prolong. of I–either to PD or V

B. i–step-descent bass leading to PD—HC

C. i–ascending ARP to phrygian cadence

PHRASE 2:

V—deceptive prog.–cadence: PAC

i–step-descent bass leading to expanded PD–PAC

i–descending ARP to extended PD–PAC

EXERCISE 18.5   Composition

Below is the accompaniment for an antecedent phrase. Write a melody to the accompaniment, and then complete an interrupted period by writing a consequent phrase.

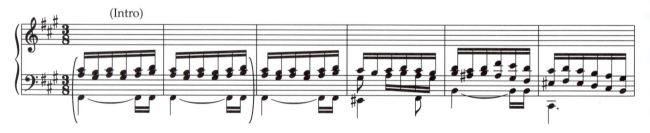

EXERCISE 18.6   Keyboard: Reduction

Sing the following excerpts from the oratorio and operatic repertory. Then, re-duce the figurated texture to a four-voice homophonic keyboard texture. Accompany your singing with your reduction. Be able to discuss each excerpt's phrase, period, or sentence structure.

A.   Mozart, "Non so più cosa son, cosa faccio," *Le nozze di Figaro* (*The Marriage of Figaro*), act 1, scene 3, K. 492

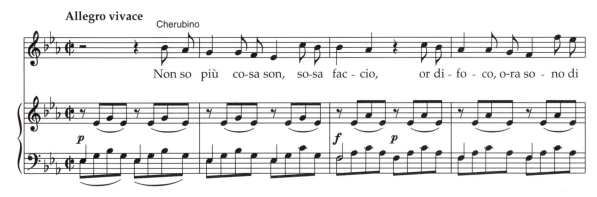

Non so più cosa son, cosa faccio,	I don't know what I'm doing any more or what I'm donig
or di fuoco, ora sono di ghiaccio,	now I'm on fire and now I'm freezing.
ogni donna cangiar di colore,	Every woman I see makes change color
ogni donna mi fa palpitar.	Every woman makes me tremble.

B.   Mozart, "Dove sono" ("Where Are They"), *Le nozze di Figaro* (*The Marriage of Figaro*), act 3, scene 8, K. 492

(Continued)

(Continued)

di _ pia — cer, _____ do — ve an-da — ro i gin — ra men — ti

di quel lab - bro men-ro - gner, di quel lab — bro men — ro-gner!

Dove sono i bei momenti
di dolcezza e di piacer,
dove andaro i giuramenti
di quel labbro menzogner?

Where are those cherished moments
of sweetness and pleasure,
Where have they gone, those vows
He so deceitfully changed?

EXERCISE 18.7 Keyboard: Harmonization

Choose three of the melodies below and determine possible harmonizations and
period types. Harmonic changes usually occur once per measure. Accompany
yourself with your harmonization.

A. Foster: "Old Folks at Home"

1. Way down up on - the Swa - nee Riv - er, Far, far a - way,

There's where my heart is turn - ing ev - er, There's where the old folks stay.

B. "Auld Lang Syne"

1. Should aul ac-quain-tance be for-got, And nev - er brought to mind? Should

auld ac-quain - tance be for-got, And _ days of auld lang syne?

C. "Red River Valley"

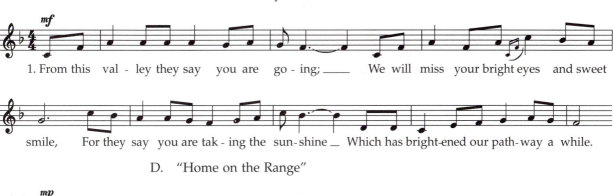

1. From this val - ley they say you are go - ing; _____ We will miss your bright eyes and sweet

smile, For they say you are tak - ing the sun - shine _ Which has bright-ened our path-way a while.

D. "Home on the Range"

1. Oh, give me a home where the buf - fa-lo roam, Where the deer and the an - te-lope play; _____

_____ Where sel-dom is heard a dis-cour - ag-ing word, And the skies are not cloud-y all day. _____

CHAPTER 19

Harmonic Sequences: Concepts and Patterns

EXERCISE 19.1 Analysis of Descending Second Sequences

 Study the following examples of D2 (D5/A4) sequences. Do not place a roman numeral beneath every chord, because the chords within a sequence are members of a linear motion and do not carry individual harmonic weight.

1. Bracket the beginning and end of each sequence.
2. Determine whether root-position chords or alternating first inversions are used. Label each sequence precisely.
3. Determine whether each copy maintains the model's voice leading precisely. Label the interval between bass and soprano in each model and in one copy.
4. Mark the location of the single tritone that occurs between IV and vii in major and ii° and VI in minor.

D.

EXERCISE 19.2   Analysis of Descending Third Sequences

Study the D3 (D4/A2) sequences below.

1. Bracket the beginning and end of each sequence.
2. Determine whether root-position chords or alternating first inversions are used. Label each sequence precisely.
3. Does each repetition maintain the model's voice leading precisely? Label the interval between bass and soprano in each model and in one repetition.

A.

B.   Chopin, Mazurka in B minor, op. 30, no. 2, B♭ 105

C.   Bach, *Gavotte*, French Suite in G major, BWV 816

EXERCISE 19.3   Analysis of Ascending Sequences

Listen to and study the following examples of A2 (A5/D4) and A2 (D3/A4) sequences as well as their $\frac{6}{3}$ variants.

A.   Mozart, *Andante*, Symphony No. 40 in G minor, K. 550

B.   Schubert, Adagio, from String Quintet in C major

C.   Handel, *Allegro*, Trio Sonata in G minor, op. 2, no. 5, HWV 390

D. Chopin, Etude in E♭ minor, op. 10, no. 6, BI 57

In spite of the intense surface chromaticism, the sequence is clear: focus on the bass and the metrically stressed beats.

EXERCISE 19.4   Aural Identification of Sequences

This exercise is the same as textbook Exercise 19.4, but now $^6_3$ variants are added to D2 (D5/A4) and D3 (D4/A2), and A2 (A5/D4) and A2 (D3/A4) sequences. Follow the listening guidelines below.

1. Determine whether the sequence ascends or descends. This step reduces sequential possibilities by 50 percent.

2. Listen to the bass to determine which one of the two remaining sequence types is played. Focus on the repetitions of the model; for example, in a descending sequence, does the bass descend by third or second? It is slightly more difficult to distinguish between the two ascending sequences given that they both ascend by second. Focus on whether you hear minimal harmonic movement; if so, it is the ascending A2 (D3/A4) sequence. If you hear a hopping bass, then it is the A2 (A5/D4) sequence.

A. _____

B. _____

C. _____

D. _____

E. _____

F. _____

G. _____

EXERCISE 19.5   Writing Sequences

Continue the following sequences, each of which begins on the tonic. The model is given, and outer voices for the first chord of the copy. Lead each sequence to a pre-dominant and close with an authentic cadence. Write bass and soprano first, filling in the tenor and alto only after you are sure that the repetitions replicate the model exactly. Use no accidentals within the sequence; these are entirely diatonic sequences. Label sequence type.

A.

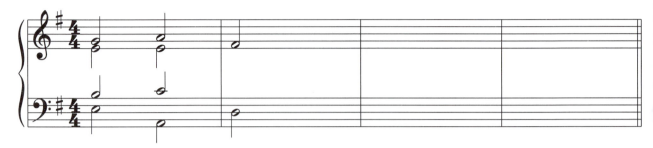

B.

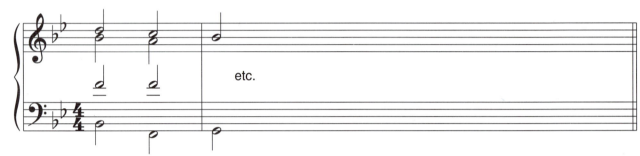

C.

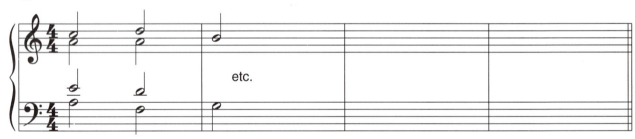

D.

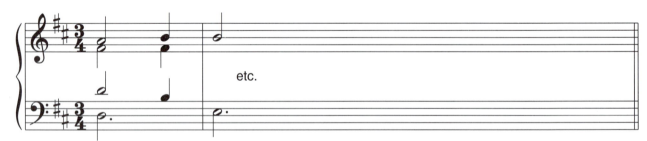

E.

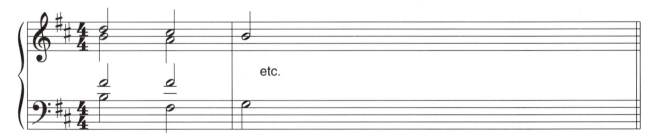

EXERCISE 19.6   Keyboard: Sequences with $^6_3$ Chords

Identify and play each of the sequence models below in major and minor keys up to and including three sharps and three flats. Voicings are given for the model. Be able to sing either outer voice while playing the other three voices.

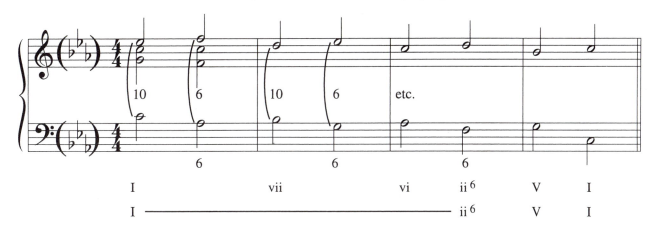

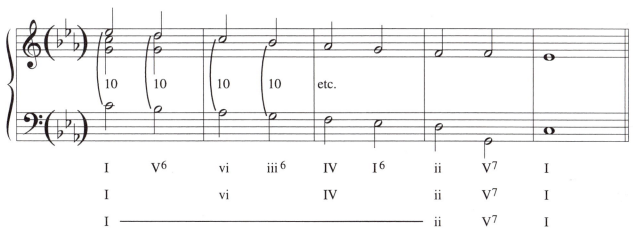

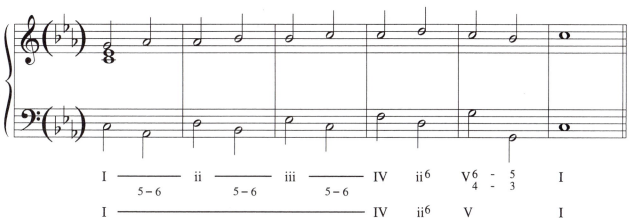

EXERCISE 19.7   Sequence Dictation

1. Label the sequence type and notate the bass for the homophonic examples.

2. Notate the soprano line. Pay close attention to the model since it determines the repetitions. Make sure that the counterpoint is logical and that pairs of intervals are consistent.

There may be a tonic expansion before the sequence begins.

A. 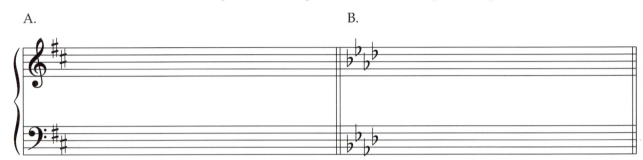 B.

C. 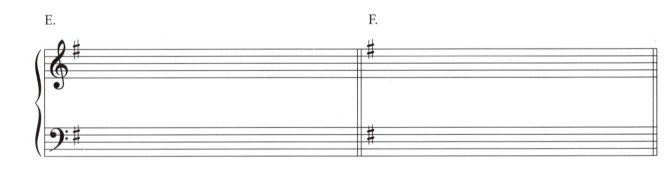 D.

E. 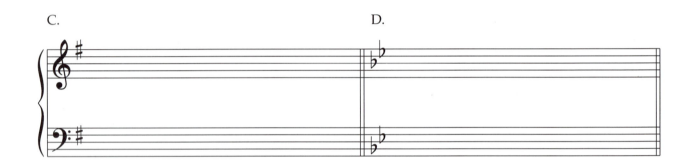 F.

G.

EXERCISE 19.8   Figured Bass and Sequences

Soprano voices are given for the following figured basses. Each example includes two or more sequences. Bracket and identify the type of sequence. (Look for the intervallic pattern that repeats every two chords.) Finally, add inner voices for the entire example and provide a two-level roman numeral analysis. Remember, do not analyze individual chords within a sequence, because they are the glue that connects the beginning and ending chords of the sequence.

A.

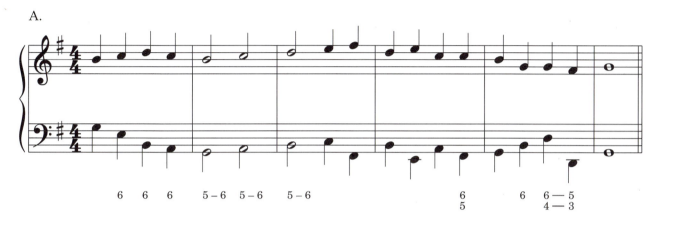

B.

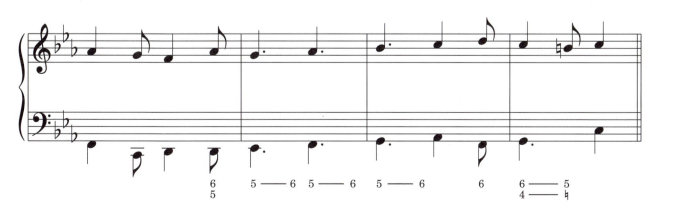

EXERCISE 19.9   Melody Harmonization

Determine the sequence type implied by the given soprano melody. Then, add a bass voice and inner voices; maintain the model's voicing in each repetition. Be able to sing either outer voice while playing the remaining three voices. Label each sequence type.

A.

Bb:

B.

g:

C.

D:

D.

b:

EXERCISE 19.10 Analysis and Notation of Sequences

Below are the incomplete scores of excerpts; the bass lines are missing. Identify the sequence type and notate the bass line in each of the excerpts. An occasional bass starting pitch is given.

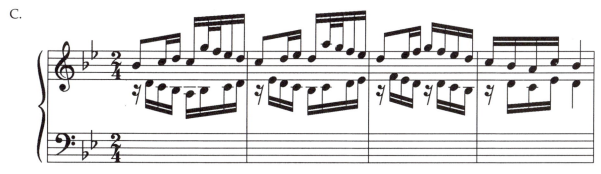

E.   Schumann, *Mit inigem Ausdruck*, Piano Trio No. 2 in F Major, op. 80

F.   Beethoven, *Rondo: Allegro molto,* Violin Sonata No. 3 in E♭ major, op. 12, no. 3

G.   Quantz, *Allegro*, Trio Sonata in G minor

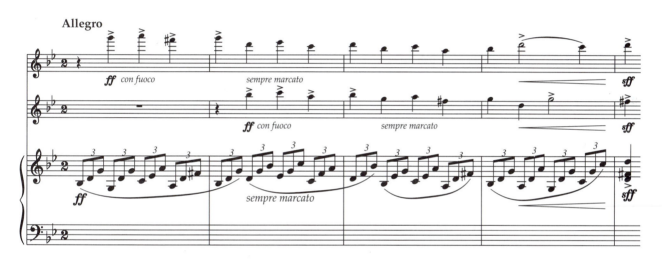

H.   Chopin, *Allegro, ma non troppo*, Mazurka in F major, op. 68, no. 3, BI 34

I.   Beethoven, *Vivace*, Piano Sonata No. 25 in G major, op. 79

J.   Corelli, *Corrente,* Concerto Grosso in C major, op. 6, no. 10

K.   Beethoven, *Vivace, ma non troppo,* Piano Sonata No. 30 in E major, op. 109

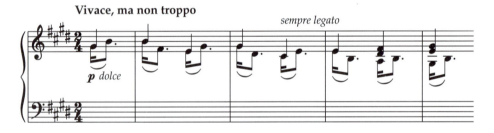

EXERCISE 19.11   Keyboard: Figured Bass

Realize the figured bass below in four voices. Label all sequences. Be able to sing the bass while playing the upper voices.

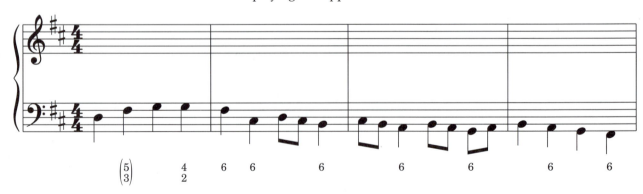

5 – 6   5 – 6   6
                                                5

EXERCISE 19.12   Keyboard: Illustrations

Choose one of the illustrations below.

A. In D minor and a meter of your choice:

1. establish tonic (*c.* 2 mm.). Include one suspension.
2. use a descending sequence that leads to an HC (*c.* 2–3 mm.).
3. begin again on tonic; use any rising sequence to lead to a cadential $^6_4$ chord. Close with a PAC.

B. In E minor and a meter of your choice:

1. establish tonic; use a voice exchange (*c.* 2 mm.).
2. use a D3 (D4/A2) sequence to lead to a PD and an IAC.
3. begin again on tonic; use an A2 (D3/A4) sequence to lead to iv.
4. close with a PAC; include one suspension.

EXERCISE 19.13   Composition

A. Realize the figured bass in the consequent phrase using the accompanimental figuration established in the beginning of the exercise. Then, compose a melody for a solo instrument or voice above the accompaniment.

B. Continue the opening of the phrase below and lead to a half cadence; then write a suitable consequent phrase to create a parallel interrupted period.

C. Brahms, "Dort in den Weiden steht ein Haus" ("There in the Willows Stands a House"), *Deutsche Volkslieder*, WoO 33, no. 31 (adapted)

Study the opening phrase of Brahms's song. Write an eight-measure continuous consequent phrase that contains a sequence and closes with a PAC. The resulting structure will be a PIP cast in sentence structure (4 + 4 + 8).

Dort in den Weiden steht ein Haus, da schaut die Magd zum Fenster 'naus! . . .

Des Morgens fährt er auf dem Fluss, und singt herüber seinen Gruss, . . .

There in the willows stands a house, and there a maiden looks out of the window! . . .

In the mornings he sails on the river and sings to me his greeting; . . .

CHAPTER 20

Sequences within Larger Musical Contexts and Sequences with Seventh Chords

EXERCISE 20.1   Analysis of Sequential Progressions and Parallel $^6_3$ Passages

Bracket and label sequences, sequential progressions, and parallel $^6_3$ chord streams. Label suspensions and determine whether the $^6_3$ chords function transitionally or prolongationally.

A.   Handel, *Gigue*, Suite XVI in G minor, HWV 263
Consider this example to be in D minor. Make a 1:1 contrapuntal reduction of the excerpt. What long-range contrapuntal event takes place between the downbeats of m. 10 and m. 12?

B.   Handel, "But Who May Abide the Day of His Coming?" *Messiah*, HWV 56
What contrapuntal technique is used at the beginning of this excerpt? Compare this example with the previous one.

C.   Schubert, German Dance No. 1, *German Dances and Ecossaises,* D. 643

D.   Corelli, *Corrente,* Concerto Grosso in C major, op. 6, no. 10

EXERCISE 20.2   Figured Bass

Realize the figured bass below, labeling all sequences. Analyze with two levels. Sequence choices are as follows:

1. D2 (D5/A4): $\frac{5}{3}$s, $\frac{6}{3}$s, sevenths (alternating or interlocking)
2. A2 (A5/D4)
3. D3 (D4/A2): $\frac{5}{3}$s or $\frac{6}{3}$s (the descending 5–6)
4. A2 (D3/A4) (the ascending 5–6 technique)

A.

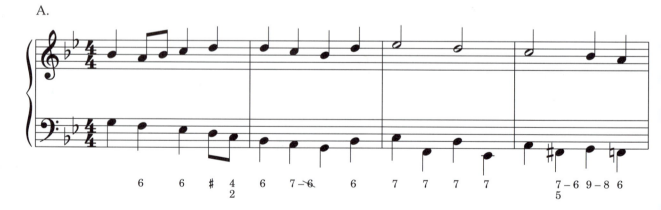

B.

EXERCISE 20.3   Completion of Sequence Patterns

Write at least two repetitions of the sequence models given below. Lead each sequence to an authentic cadence. Analyze. Then, rewrite each completed sequence by adding at least one tone of figuration (e.g., suspension, passing tone) to the model and its copies.

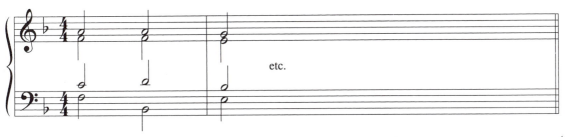

(Continued)

(*Continued*)

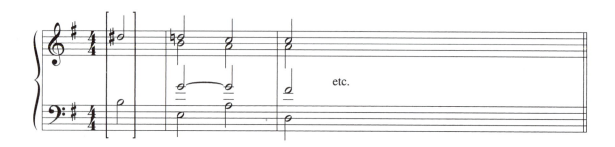

EXERCISE 20.4   Illustrations

Complete the following tasks in four-voice SATB style.

A. In D minor, write a four-measure phrase that includes the following:

  1. a D2 (D5/A4) sequence leading to an HC
  2. at least three suspensions
  3. a neighboring and cadential $^6_4$ chord

B. In B♭ major, write a four-measure phrase that includes the following:

  1. a contrapuntal expansion of tonic
  2. a D3 (D4/A2) sequence
  3. a bass suspension
  4. a bass arpeggiation
  5. a submediant harmony
  6. a deceptive progression

C. In C minor, write a four-measure phrase that includes the following:

  1. a D2 (D5/A4) sequence with interlocking sevenths
  2. passing tones

D. In A major, write a four-measure phrase that includes the following:

  1. an A2 (D3/A4) sequence (ascending 5–6)
  2. a deceptive progression
  3. two suspensions
  4. a neighboring $^6_4$ chord

EXERCISE 20.5   Analysis and Notation

The following sequences from the literature are missing bass lines. Listen to and study each sequence; then, identify each sequence and notate the bass line. Example G contains more than one sequence.

A. Mozart, *Allegro,* Piano Sonata in F Major, K. 332
Consider this excerpt to be in C minor. What rhythmic device is employed in mm. 64 and 65?

B. Chopin, Etude in G♭ major, op. 25

C. Haydn, *Moderato,* Piano Sonata No. 44 in B♭ major, Hob. XVI. 29

D. Geminiani, Violin Sonata, op. 1, No. 12

E. Bach, *Allemande,* English Suite No. 3 in G minor, BWV 808

F. Corelli, *Allegro,* Concerto Grosso in F major, op. 6, no. 2

G.   Tchaikovsky, Andantino in mododi canzona, Symphony No. 4

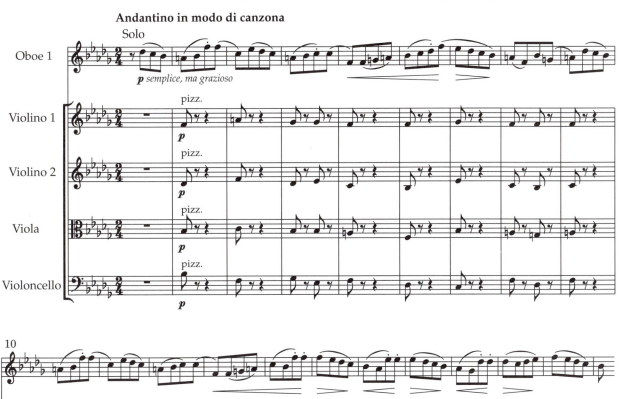

H.   Corelli, *Gigue: Allegro*, Concerto Grosso in F major, op. 6, no. 12

(Continued)

(*Continued*)

EXERCISE 20.6　Notation of Sequences

You will hear several D2 (D5/A4) sequences with and without sevenths. You are to do the following:

1. determine whether the sequence contains alternating or interlocking sevenths
2. notate the bass

A.

B.

C.

D.　Handel: "Pena tiranna io sento" from *Amadigi di gaula*; act 1

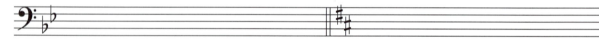

E.　Bach, *Menuet II*, French Suite in D minor, BWV 812.
Measures 1–8 contain a sequential harmonic progression. Do not notate the bass for these measures; merely identify the sequential progression. Measures 9–16 are strictly sequential; notate the primary bass note in each measure. What is the harmonic relationship between the first and second eight-measure units?

F.　Schumann, "Ich will meine Seele tauchen" ("I Want to Delve my Soul"), *Dichterliebe*, op. 48, no. 5. You will hear the entire song, which is composed of two large phrases. Each phrase may in turn be divided into two subphrases. What type of larger musical structure do the two large phrases create? Each large phrase begins unusually with a pre-dominant harmony, ii$^{\varnothing}_7$, rather than the tonic.

EXERCISE 20.7　Conversion

Reduce the excerpts below to homophonic four-voice textures. Then, convert the descending $^6_3$ passages into D2 (D5/A4) sequences with seventh chords. A worked solution appears below.

Sample Solution

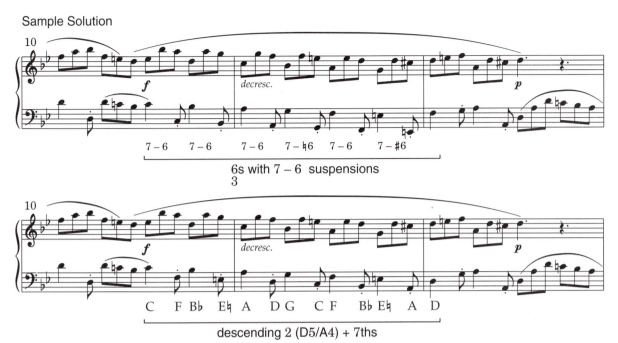

A. Corelli, *Allemanda: Allegro,* Concerto Grosso in C major, op. 6, no. 10

B. Corelli, *Corrente,* Concerto Grosso in C major, op. 6, no. 10

C.   Haydn, *Finale: Tempo di Minuet,* Piano Sonata No. 37 in E major, Hob. XVI. 22

EXERCISE 20.8   Analysis

 Analyze the examples below that contain D2 (D5/A4) sequences with inverted seventh chords. Circle each chordal seventh and label its preparation and resolution.

A.   Leclair, *Sarabanda,* Trio Sonata in D major, op. 2, no. 8

B.   Marcello, *Largo,* Trio Sonata in B♭ major, op. 2, no. 2
Focus on the continuo realization.

EXERCISE 20.9   Figured Bass

Realize the figured bass below; bracket and label sequences. Provide a roman numeral analysis for all harmonies outside of the sequences. Inverted seventh chords must be complete.

EXERCISE 20.10   Comparison of Sequential Passages from the Literature

Below are three examples from Mozart's *Magic Flute*. Listen to each and then in a short paragraph, compare and contrast their content. Include in your discussion not only specific types of sequences but also their functions within the larger musical context.

Mozart's *Die Zauberflöte* (*The Magic Flute*), K. 620

A.   "Drei Knäbchen" (Three Little Boys"), act I, scene 9

Drei Knäbchen, jung, schön, hold ,   Three boys, young, pretty, good,
    und weise   and wise
Umschweben euch auf eurer Reise.   Will hover near you on your journey.

B.   "Holle Rache" ("Hell's Revenge"), act 2, scene 8

C. "Wie, wie, wie?" ("What, What, What?"), act 2, scene 5

Wie, wie, wie?   What? What? What?
Ihr an diesem Schreckensort?   You in this place of dread?
Nie, nie, nie   Never, never, never
Kommt ihr wieder glücklich fort!   Will you come out again!

EXERCISE 20.11 Melody Harmonization and Sequences

Based on the contour of the following soprano fragments, determine an appropriate sequence type and then harmonize each in four voices (SATB). Examples A–D require one chord change for each melody note. Examples E–F contain tones of figuration and are incomplete. For these, determine the larger sequential pattern, add the sequential bass, and complete the sequence and lead to a cadence. Label each sequence type. A sample solution appears below.

Solution

(Continued)

(*Continued*)

A.

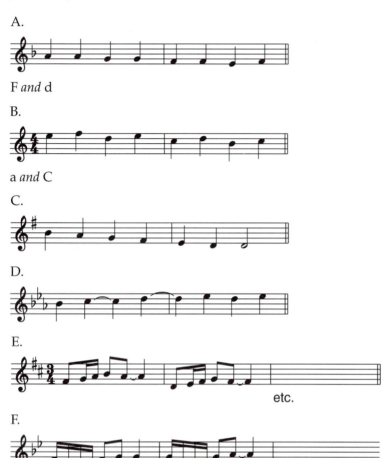

F *and* d

B.

a *and* C

C.

D.

E.

etc.

F.

etc.

EXERCISE 20.12   Analysis of Sequences Appearing in Compound Melodies

Determine the sequence type in the compound melodies below and then provide a reductive verticalization of the implied voices (either three or four).

Sample Solution

44

A2

A.   Bach, *Menuet*, French Suite in B minor, BWV 814. Bracket subphrases in this example. What type of formal structure occurs?

B. Schumann, *Kreisleriana*, op. 16, no. 5
While not strictly a compound melody, it is possible to create a five-voice structure.

C. Bach, *Menuet*, French Suite in C minor, BWV 813

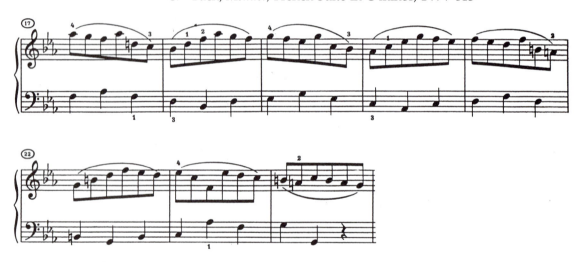

EXERCISE 20.13   Aural Identification of Sequences within Phrases

Notate the bass of the incomplete scores and provide a roman numeral analysis.
Bracket and label sequences.

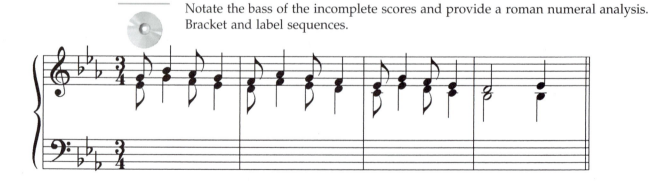

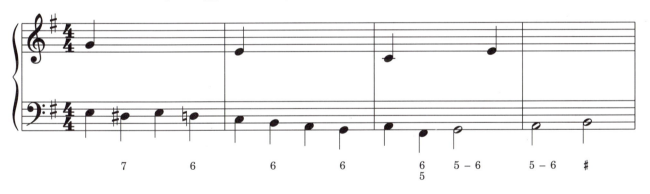

EXERCISE 20.14   Keyboard: Figured Bass

Realize the figured bass in four voices; a few given soprano pitches will guide your upper line. Sing the bass voice while playing the upper parts. Analyze.

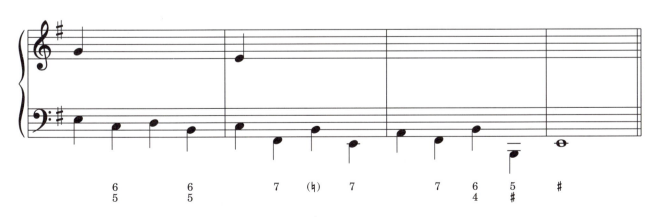

EXERCISE 20.15   Expansion of Basic Progressions

 You will hear two basic chord progressions; each is followed by elaborated versions that include contrapuntal expansions and sequences. Notate the bass and the soprano and include roman numerals. In a sentence or two, describe the way the tonic is expanded.

Model 1:

Expansion #1: (3 mm)   Expansion #2: (3 mm)

Expansion #3: (3 mm)   Expansion #4: (4 mm)

Model 2: (all expansions occupy four measures)

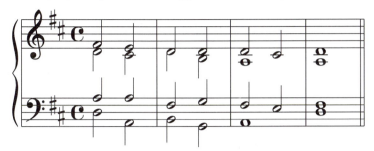

Expansion #1:

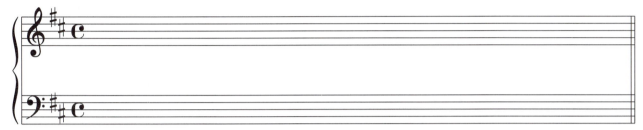

Expansion #2:

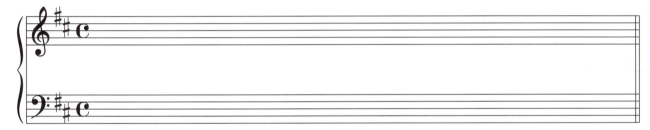

Expansion #3:

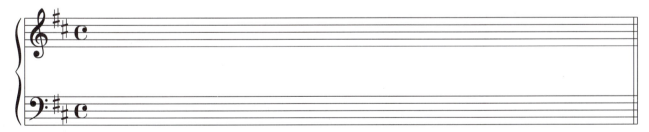

Expansion #4:

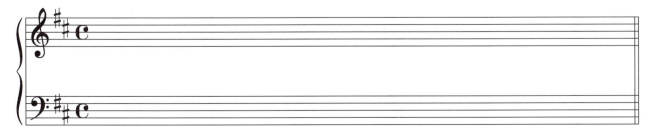

CHAPTER 21

Applied Chords

EXERCISE 21.1 Aural Comparison of Progressions with and without Applied Chords

You will hear four pairs of short progressions; the first progression of the pair is diatonic and the second adds applied chords that embellish the first progression. Listen to the model and write out the roman numerals. Then, listen to the second example, each of which contains one applied chord. For each applied chord you hear, write "V" beneath the harmony and follow it with an arrow that leads to the diatonic chord that is being tonicized. For example, if the first progression you hear is I–V–I, but the second contains an applied chord between the tonic and the dominant, you would write I–V–V–I.

A. model: ___ ___ ___

___ ___ ___ ___

B. model: ___ ___ ___ ___

___ ___ ___ ___ ___

C. model: ___ ___ __

___ ___ ___ ___

D. model: ___ ___ ___ ___

___ ___ ___ ___ ___

EXERCISE 21.2 Recognizing Applied Chords: Analysis

The examples below contain applied chords: V(7)/ii, V(7)/III, V7/IV, V(7)/V, and V(7)/vi. All are possible in both major and minor keys except for V/ii in minor. Remember that dissonant triads such as iio cannot be tonicized. For each excerpt:

1. analyze all diatonic chords with roman numerals and give a second-level analysis.
2. circle and label each applied chord with a roman numeral.

A sample analysis has been given. Remember to use your eye and ear to pinpoint new chromatic tones and harmonies foreign to the key.

Mozart, *Trio*, String Quartet in E♭ major, K. 171

A.

B.

C.

D.

E.   Schubert, Waltz in B♭ major, *German Dances and Ecossaises*, D. 783

EXERCISE 21.3   Error Detection of Applied Chords

Below are notated and analyzed applied triads and Mm seventh chords. The last five examples include resolution of the applied chord.

Exercises A–E: Assume the roman numeral analysis and given key to be correct. Renotate incorrect pitches in each chord in order to conform to the roman numerals.

Exercises F–J: Assume the notated pitches and given key to be correct. Change incorrect roman numerals in order to conform to the notated pitches and given key.

Exercises K–O: Assume the roman numerals and given key to be correct. Renotate pitches in the applied chord and its resolution to conform to the analysis, the given key, and correct voice leading.

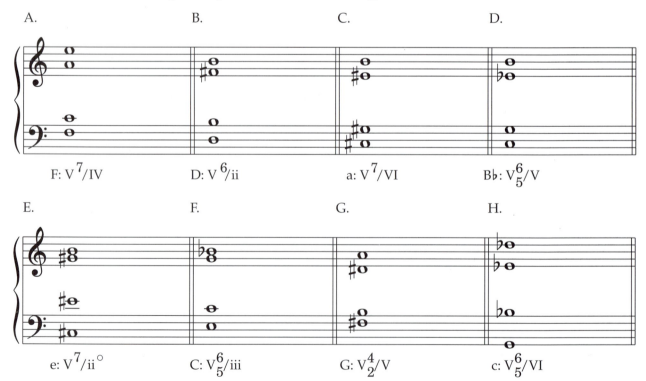

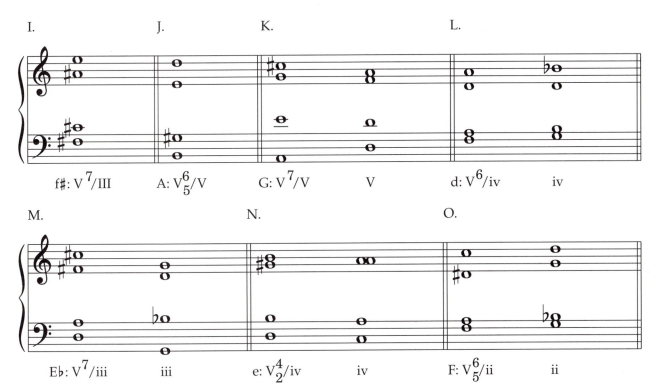

I.   J.   K.   L.

f#: V^7/III   A: V$^6_5$/V   G: V^7/V   V   d: V^6/iv   iv

M.   N.   O.

Eb: V^7/iii   iii   e: V$^4_2$/iv   iv   F: V$^6_5$/ii   ii

EXERCISE 21.4   Resolving Applied Chords

Analyze each applied chord according to the given key, then lead each to its respective tonic, resolving all tendency tones correctly. Example K is longer and requires you to notate both the applied chord and its resolution. Analyze.

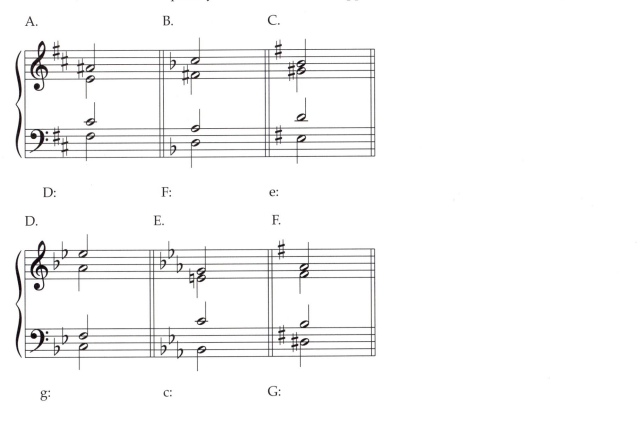

A.   B.   C.

D: F: e:

D.   E.   F.

g: c: G:

d: f#:   E♭:   B♭:

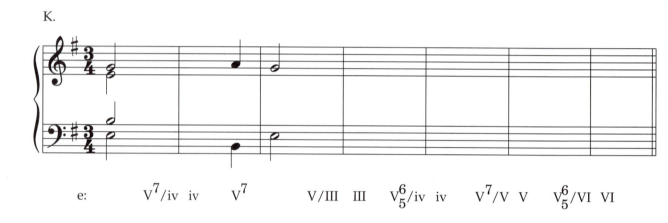

e: V⁷/iv iv   V⁷   V/III III   V⁶₅/iv iv   V⁷/V V   V⁶₅/VI VI

EXERCISE 21.5   Figured Bass with Given Soprano

The figured bass below incorporates applied chords. Fill in the inner voices and analyze using two levels.

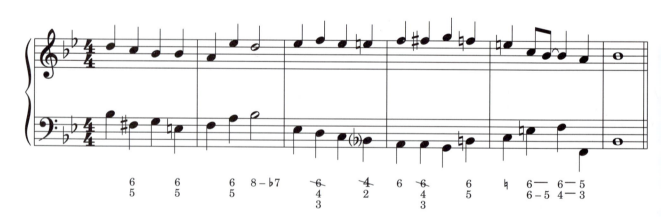

EXERCISE 21.6   Keyboard: Model Progressions

Play in major and minor modes as specified in keys up to and including two sharps and two flats. Be able to sing either outer voice while playing the remaining three voices. Analyze.

EXERCISE 21.7   Keyboard Brain Twister

Based on the given key signature determine the roman numeral for each given chord in both a major key and its relative minor. Then, play and resolve each applied chord. Finally, close each example with a cadence in the major key and the relative minor key.

EXERCISE 21.8   Figured Bass

Realize the figured basses that include applied vii°6 and vii°7 chords. The soprano is given. Provide a two-level analysis.

A.

B.

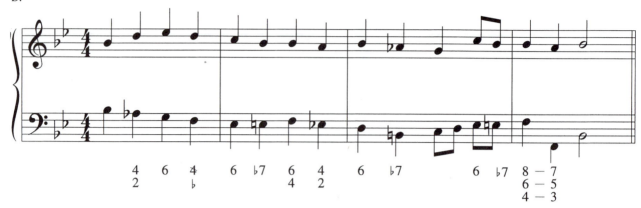

EXERCISE 21.9 Writing Applied vii°6 and vii°7

1. Complete the applied chords and resolve them, then compose an ending to the progression following the instructions preceding each example.
2. Provide a two-level analysis.

A.

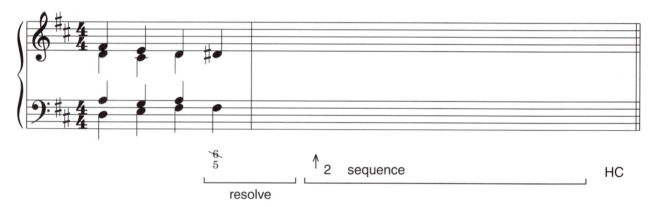

After resolving the applied chord, continue, using an A2 (D3/A4) + $\frac{6}{3}$ sequence (ascending 5–6 sequence) that leads to the dominant. Include two additional applied chords in this progression.

B.

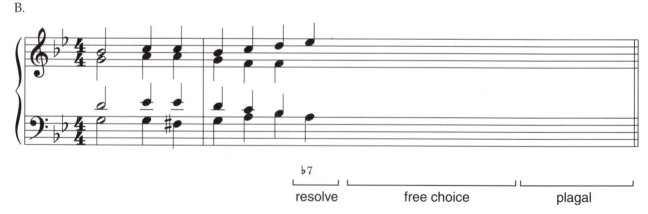

After resolving the applied chord, continue the progression for at least two measures using harmonies of your choice. There must be at least two added applied chords. Close with a plagal cadence

C.

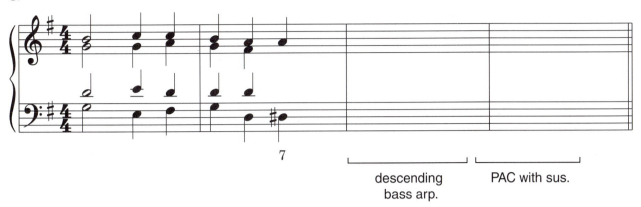

descending
bass arp.

PAC with sus.

After you resolve the applied chords, include a descending bass arpeggiation;
close with a PAC that includes a suspension.

D.

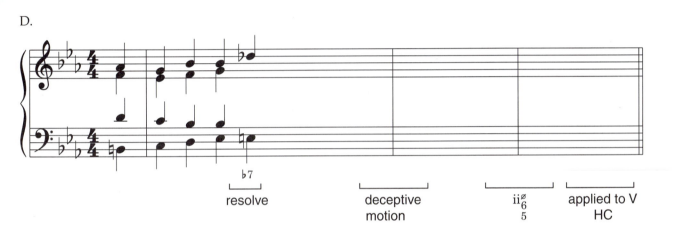

resolve

deceptive
motion

ii$^{\varnothing 6}_{5}$

applied to V
HC

After resolving the applied chord, include a deceptive harmonic motion followed
by ii$^{\varnothing 6}_{5}$. Close with a half cadence; use an applied dominant seventh to precede
the final dominant harmony.

EXERCISE 21.10   Keyboard: Short Progressions

Play the following progressions:

In G major and B♭ major: I–V$^6_5$/IV–IV
In G major and B♭ major: I–V7/ii–ii
In G major and B♭ major: V–V$^6_5$/vi–vi
In D major and F major: I–V$^4_3$/vi–vi–V$^6_5$/V–V
In A minor and E minor: i–V$^6_5$/III–III–V$^6_5$/iv–v–vii°7/V–V

EXERCISE 21.11   Notation of Chromatic Tones

Below are notated diatonic progressions, to which applied chords will be added.
Notate appropriate pitches and roman numerals that reflect these added applied
harmonies.

Listening tip: Remember, a chromatically raised pitch functions as the temporary leading tone to the next chord (i.e., it becomes $\hat{7}$), and a chromatically lowered pitch usually functions as the seventh of the chord that descends to the third of the following chord. The chromaticism often appears in an outer voice.

A.

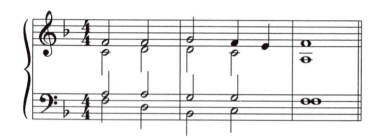

B.

C.   Note the parallel fifths between bass and tenor in m. 1. Recall that added applied chords are often used as voice-leading correctives that eliminate such fifths and octaves.

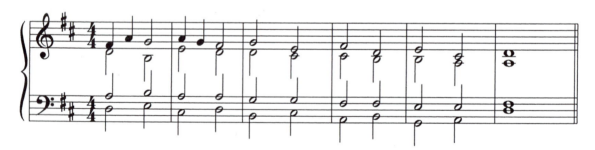

D.

E.

F.

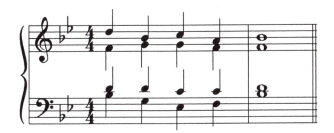

EXERCISE 21.12 Analysis: Applied Chords within Phrases and Periods

Below are examples from the literature. Provide roman numerals (use two levels of analysis) and answer any questions on a separate piece of paper.

A. Beethoven, *Allegro* and *Adagio cantabile,* Piano Trio No. 1 in E♭ major, op. 1

1. In a sentence or two, discuss the phrase structure of the first passage. Is it a single phrase, a period, independent phrases, or some other structure?
2. Label the period type in the second excerpt.
3. Compare and contrast the harmonic structure of the two excerpts.

A1.

Note the $^6_4$ chord in m. 2; does it function as you would expect a $^6_4$ chord to function? (Hint: Is there an underlying progression in mm. 1 through 4?)

A2.

B. Mozart, "Agnus Dei," *Requiem*, K. 626
    Do the chords in mm. 3 and 5 function harmonically or contrapuntally?

C.   Mozart, *Allegro,* String Quartet in F major, K. 158

D.   Elgar, "Salut d'Amour" ("Love's Greeting"), op. 12
Make a phrase/period diagram.

E.   Haydn, *Allegro con spirito*, String Quartet in B♭ major, op. 76, no. 4, Hob. III. 78
Is this a single phrase or a period? Support your answer.

EXERCISE 21.13   Comparison of Applied Chords: Dominant
Seventh Versus Diminished Seventh

Differentiate between dominant seventh and diminished seventh applied chords.
Then, notate the bass and the soprano voices and provide roman numerals.

A.   B.

C.

D.   E.

EXERCISE 21.14   Figured Bass

Fill in the inner voices and analyze using two levels. Watch for added chromaticism.

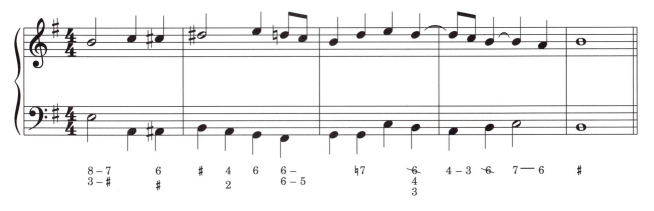

8 – 7	6	4	6	6 –	♮7	6	4 – 3	6	7 — 6	♯
3 – ♯	♯	2		6 – 5		4				
						3				

EXERCISE 21.15   Harmonizing Melodic Fragments with Applied Chords

In a logical meter and rhythmic setting of your choice, harmonize the melodic fragments using applied chords. Arrows indicate applied chord placement. Your harmonic progression should make sense. Analyze.

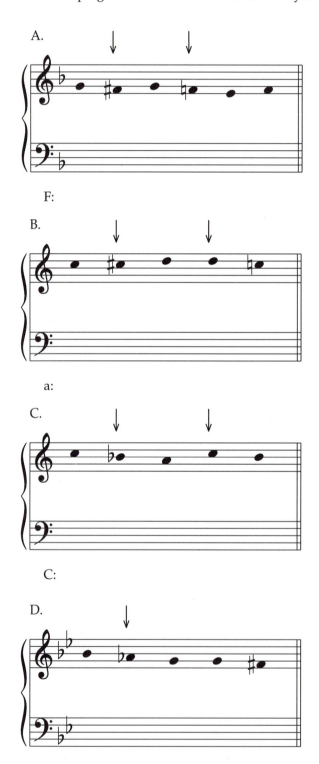

Bb:

b:

EXERCISE 21.16 Figured Bass

Write a soprano line and inner voices, and analyze using two levels.

(Continued)

(Continued)

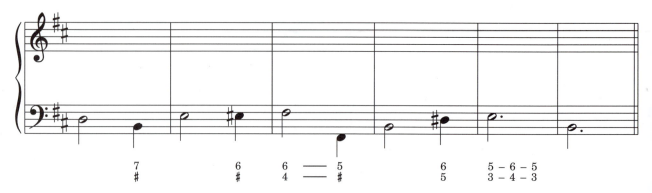

EXERCISE 21.17   Keyboard: Figured Bass

Realize the figured bass below. Add inner voices and analyze with two levels.

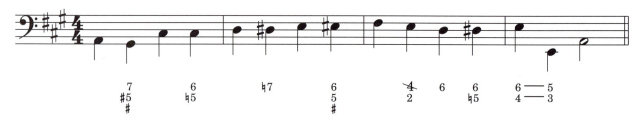

EXERCISE 21.18   Writing Phrases, Periods, and Sentences

Construct periods in four voices based on the instructions below. Analyze and label each of the required elements.

A.   In G major, write an eight-measure parallel interrupted period that contains the following:

1.   at least two applied chords in its first phrase
2.   at least two suspensions in its second phrase
3.   one example of a neighboring, cadential, and passing $^6_4$ chord in one of the two phrases

B.   In B minor, write an eight-measure parallel interrupted period that contains the following:

1.   one D3 (D4/A2) sequence (may include the $^6_3$ form)
2.   a bass suspension and at least three passing tones
3.   two examples of applied diminished seventh chords in one of the two phrases

C.   In G minor, write an eight-measure parallel sectional period that contains the following:

1.   any sequence
2.   an inverted applied dominant seventh chord
3.   a cadential $^6_4$
4.   two accented passing tones

D.   In C minor, write an eight-measure sentence that contains the following:

1.   a step-descent bass
2.   an ascending bass arpeggiation
3.   two examples of applied diminished seventh chords

E.   In E♭ major, write an eight-measure contrasting continuous period that contains the following:

1.   an A2 (D4/A3) sequence (or its $\frac{6}{3}$ variant)
2.   a deceptive progression
3.   a suspension, accented passing tone, appoggiatura, and neighbor
4.   a descending bass arpeggiation

EXERCISE 21.19   Analysis: Identification of Applied Chord Sequences

 Listen to and analyze each excerpt, marking the beginning and ending points of each sequence. Next, identify the sequence type by label. Finally, provide roman numerals for the remaining chords in each example.

A.

B.

C.

D.

E. Vivaldi, *Allegro,* Concerto Grosso in F major, op. 9, no. 11, Ry198A, Fi133, F.I/58, P416

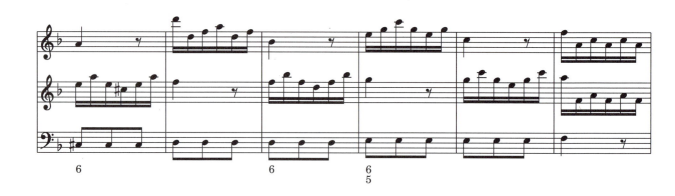

EXERCISE 21.20   Applied Chord Sequences within the Phrase Model: Analysis and Notation

You will hear four phrases from the literature that contain applied chord sequences. The upper voices are provided.

1. Identify the sequence and notate the bass line.
2. Provide a two-level analysis of the excerpt.

A. Mozart, *Minuetto,* String Quartet in B♭ major ("Hunt"), K. 458

B. Schubert, Waltz in G major, *Twelve German Dances and Five Ecossaises*, D. 529, no. 3

C. Schubert, Waltz in A major, *Twelve German Dances and Five Ecossaises*, D. 420, no. 12

D. Beethoven, *Adagio molto expressivo*, Violin Sonata No. 6 in A major, op. 30, no. 1
Note that there is a slightly longer tonicization of each step within the sequence.

EXERCISE 21.21   Completing Applied Chord Sequences

Determine the type of applied chord sequence, then continue the sequence and cadence. Begin by writing the diatonic chords, then insert the appropriate preceding applied chord.

A.

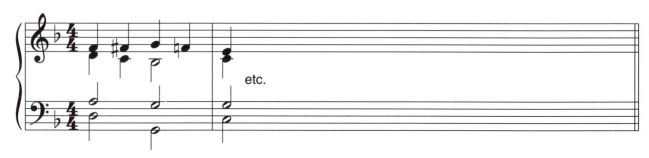

B.

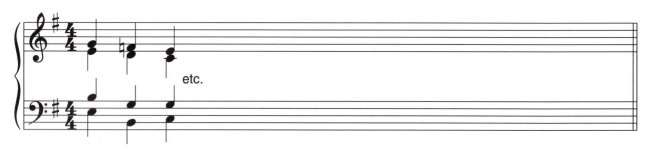

C.

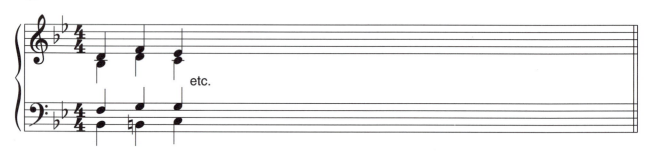

D.

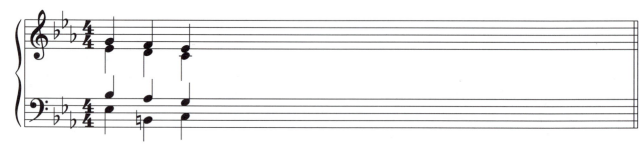

E.

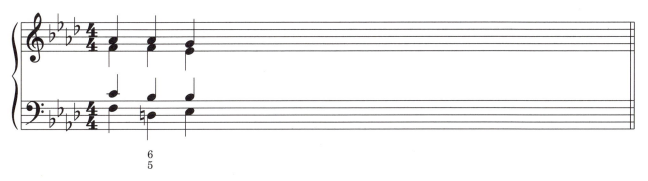

F.

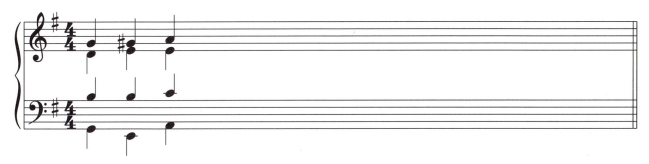

EXERCISE 21.22   Figured Bass

The figured bass below includes at least one applied chord sequence or sequential progression. Add roman numerals and inner voices.

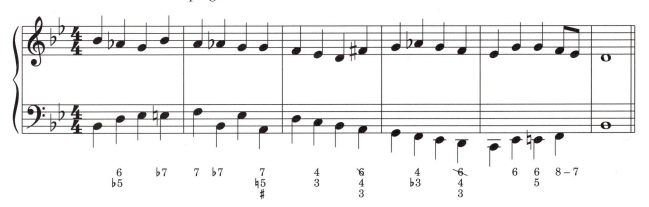

EXERCISE 21.23   Harmonizing Bass Lines

Harmonize each bass line below, which implies a diatonic or applied chord sequence. Determine a suitable meter; you may choose the note values. Analyze.

A.

F:

B.

A:

C.

b:

D.

c:

EXERCISE 21.24   Notation of Applied Chord Sequences

 Add the missing bass voice using your ear and the visual clues provided by the given upper voices. Label the sequence type.

A.

B.

C.

D.

E.

EXERCISE 21.25   Figured Bass

The figured basses below (without soprano) include multiple applied chord sequences. Write a soprano voice, analyze, and add inner voices.

1.

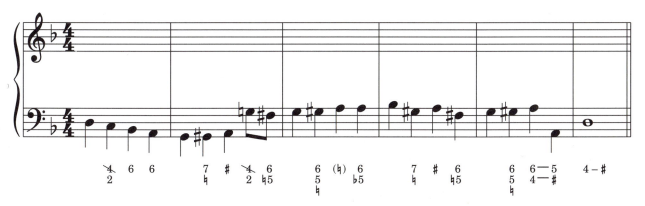

2.

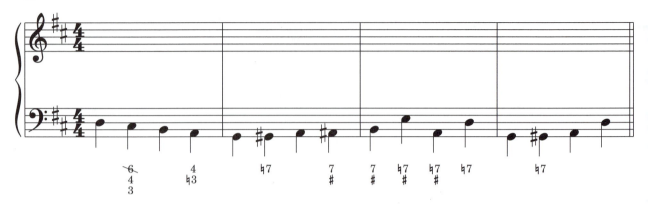

EXERCISE 21.26   Illustrations

Complete the tasks below in four voices; analyze.

A.   In C minor, write a D3 (D4/A2) sequence that incorporates root-position applied diminished seventh chords. Close with a PAC.

B.   In A major, write an A2 (D3/A4) with $^6_3$s with applied chords and an applied D2 (D5/A4) sequence with 7ths (interlocking or alternating). Close with an IAC.

C.   In G major, write a parallel interrupted period that includes the following:

1.   any applied chord sequence
2.   a deceptive progression
3.   two suspensions

D.   In B minor, write a progression that includes the following, but not necessarily in that order:

1.   an IAC
2.   an applied chord D2 (D5/A4) sequence using dominant seventh chords (alternating or interlocking)
3.   a neighboring and passing $^6_4$ chord
4.   a phrygian cadence
5.   a bass suspension
6.   a tonic expansion

EXERCISE 21.27   Keyboard: Unfigured Bass

Realize the unfigured bass in four voices. Write in a two-level analysis. Sing either outer voice while playing the other three.

CHAPTER 22

Tonicization and Modulation

EXERCISE 22.1   Analysis

Below are excerpts from the literature in which a nontonic harmony is expanded through tonicization. You are to do the following:

1. Listen to each phrase and bracket the expanded harmony.
2. Provide a detailed, chord-by-chord analysis of the harmonies within the expansion.
3. Provide a second-level analysis that places the tonicized area within the overall harmonic progression of the entire passage.

A.   Mendelssohn, *Allegro arioso*, Cello Sonata No. 1 in B♭ major, op. 45

B1, 2. Corelli, *Adagio*, Concerto Grosso, op. 6, nos. 9 and 11
Below are two *Adagio* sections from two Corelli concertos. Analyze and in a short paragraph, compare and contrast their harmonic content.

1.

2.   Consider this example to be in G minor.

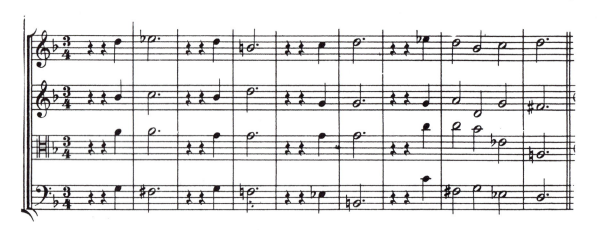

C.   Schumann, "Du bist wie eine Blume" ("You Are So Like a Flower"), *Myrten*, op. 25, no. 24

Du bist wie eine Blume,   You are so like a flower,
So hold und schön und rein;   So pure, and fair, and kind,

D. Schumann, "Talismane," *Myrten,* op. 25, no. 8

Got - tes ist der O - ri - ent!   Got - tes ist der Oc - ci -

dent!   Nord - und süd - li - ches Ge - län - de   ruht im Frie - den sei - ner Hän - de.

Gottes ist der Orient!	The Orient is God's!
Gottes ist der Occident!	The Occident is God's!
Nord und südliches Gelände	Northern and southern lands
Ruht im Frieden seiner Hände	Repose in the peace of His hands.

E. Schumann, *Mit feuer,* Piano Trio in D major, op. 63

(Continued)

(Continued)

F.　Bellini, "Casta on Diva" from *Norma*, Act I, scene 4, cavatino

EXERCISE 22.2　Figured Bass and Tonicized Areas

In order to realize the figured basses, you will need to determine which non-tonic harmonies are extended. Begin by studying the bass and figures. The appearance of chromaticism in the figures and the bass will help you.

1. Bracket each tonicized area and represent its relation to the main tonic by using a roman numeral.
2. Add upper voices and a first-level roman numeral analysis that relates each of the chords within a tonicization to the expanded harmony.

EXERCISE 22.3 Soprano Harmonization

Harmonize each soprano fragment below in three different ways. Try to incorporate applied chords, diatonic and applied chord sequences, and tonicized areas. Begin by breaking up the melodies into harmonic cells.

A.

EXERCISE 22.4 Analysis of Tonicized Areas and Modulations

The following progressions contain either tonicized areas (which close in their original key) or modulations (which close in a new key, though they may also contain tonicized areas). Use brackets to identify tonicized areas, with the roman numeral of the temporary tonal area shown below the bracket. Identify a single underlying tonal progression in examples that contain tonicized areas. Use pivots to show modulations (modulations in this exercise—though they contain pivots and demonstrate closure in a new tonal area—are artificial, given their necessary brevity). Analyze each example with two levels of roman numerals.

A.

B.

C. Beethoven, *Mit Lebhaftigkeit und durchaus mit Empfindung und Ausdruck,* Piano Sonata No. 27 in E minor, op. 90

D.

E.   Schubert, Ballet music from *Rosamunde*, D. 797

EXERCISE 22.5   Key Choices

List the closely related keys to each of the given keys. Review the various ways you can determine closely related keys.

D major _ _ _ _ _   F minor _ _ _ _ _

A♭ major _ _ _ _ _   C♯ minor _ _ _ _ _

B minor _ _ _ _ _   D♭ major _ _ _ _ _

B♭ major _ _ _ _ _

EXERCISE 22.6 Modulating Figured Basses

Realize the short figured basses below in four voices. Then analyze, being sure to label pivot chords fully.

A.

B.

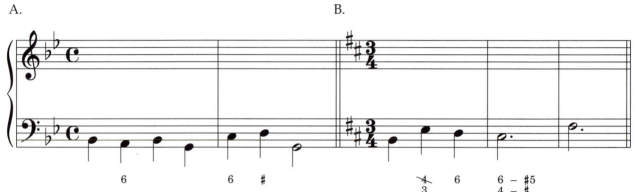

C.

D.

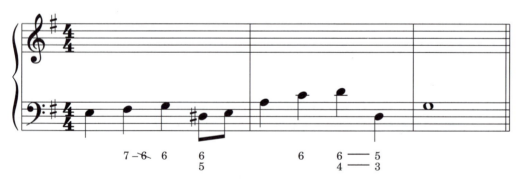

E.

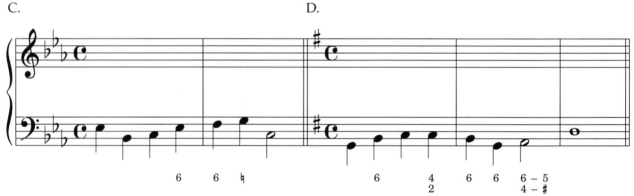

F.

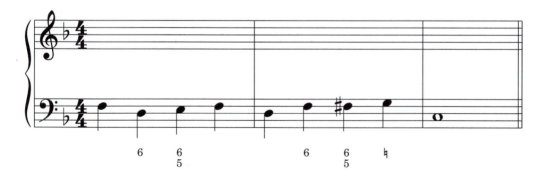

G.

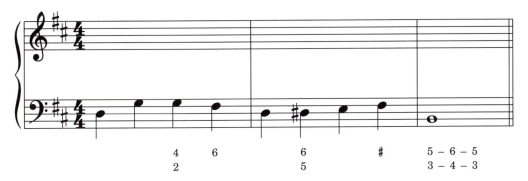

4   6   6   #   5 – 6 – 5
2   5   3 – 4 – 3

H.

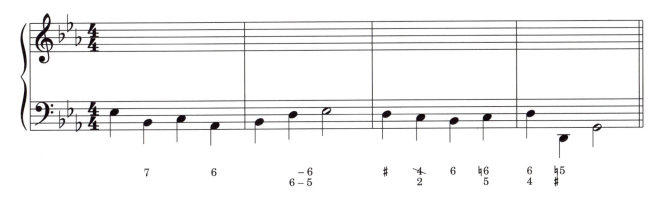

7   6   – 6   #   4   6   ♮6   6   ♮5
                    6 – 5   2   5   4   #

EXERCISE 22.7   Keyboard: Multiple Tonal Destinations

Below is the opening of a phrase and its continuation that leads to three different keys. Play each progression and analyze.

1. Determine the relationship of the new key to the old key, using roman numerals.
2. Determine the pivot chord and box it, showing original and new keys.

EXERCISE 22.8   Keyboard: Modulating Sopranos

Determine the implied initial key and the new key of each soprano fragment. Accidentals will narrow your choices considerably, but it is possible that a diatonic melody
modulates without accidentals; thus, there may be more than one harmonic interpretation. Write out the bass line of the cadence and the preceding pre-dominant.
Determine a possible bass for the opening of the progression. You will most likely
end up in the approximate middle of the fragment, and the one or two unharmo-
nized soprano pitches will be your modulatory pivot. Analyze and add inner voices.

A.   B.

C.   D.

E.

EXERCISE 22.9   Notation of Modulating Phrases and Pivot
Chord Location

Each short progression modulates, closing with a PAC. Before listening, determine modulatory possibilities. This is important because successful development
of aural and analytical skills depends not only on active processing of what is
seen and heard, but also on knowledge of normative procedures, which develops
musical expectations. By using expectations, the number of possibilities is greatly
reduced and you can then focus on just a handful of logical solutions.

An incomplete score is given for each example. Add missing bass and soprano
pitches and provide roman numerals; mark the pivot chord.

A.

B.

C.

D.

E.

F.

EXERCISE 22.10   Keyboard: Improvising Modulating Consequents

Work out a modulating consequent phrase that continues musical ideas presented in the antecedent phrase. The result will be a parallel progressive period. After studying each of the three antecedent phrases, begin the consequent in the same way that the antecedent began, but you will insert a pivot chord approximately halfway through the consequent and cadence in the new key.

A. Emilie Zumsteeg, "Nachruf" ("Farewell"), op. 6, no. 6

1. Nur ei - ne laß von dei nen-Ga - ben, ver schwund-ne-Lie - be,＿ mir＿ zu - rück!

Nur eine lass von deinen Gaben,　　　Only leave one gift with me,
Verschwundne Liebe, mir zurück!　　　Vanished love, return to me!

B. Mozart, "Sehnsuch nach dem Frühlinge" ("Longing for Spring"), K. 596

Fröhlich

1. Komm, lie - ber Mai, und ma - che die Bäu - me wie - der grün,

Komm, lieber Mai, und mache　　　Come, dear May, and make
Die Baume wieder grün　　　　　　the trees green again,

C. Clara Schumann, "Cavatina," *Variations de Concert sur la Cavatine du "Pirate" di Bellini*, op. 8

Andantino
molto espressivo

sempre piano il Basso.

EXERCISE 22.11　Dictation of Longer Modulating Phrases

Notate bass and soprano for Examples A–C and bass only for Examples D–K. Provide a roman numeral analysis and label the pivot chord.

A.

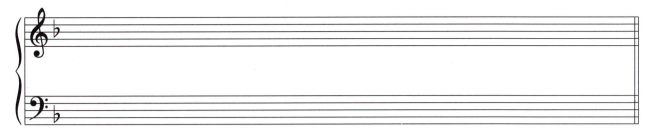

B.

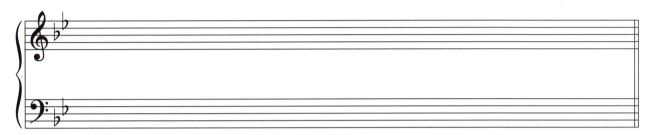

C.

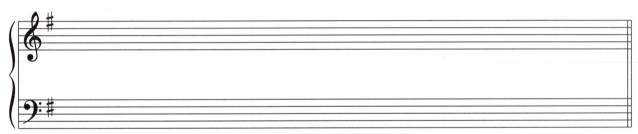

D.   Handel, *Allegro,* Concerto Grosso in C minor, op. 6, no. 8, HWV 326

E.   Mozart, "In diesen heil'gen hallen," *Die Zauberflöte (The Magic Flute),* act II, scene 3, K. 620

F.   Haydn, *Adagio,* String Quartet in C major, op. 54, no. 2, Hob. III. 58

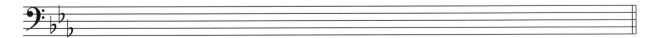

G. Schubert, Waltz in B minor, *38 Waltzes, Ländler, and Ecossaises,* D. 145

H. Beethoven, *Lustig-Traurig,* WoO 54

I. Haydn, *Allegro,* String Quartet in F major, op. 74, no. 2, Hob. III. 70

J. Chopin, Mazurka in A minor, op. 7, no. 2, BI 61

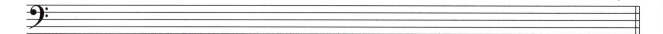

K. Haydn, *Trio,* Piano Sonata in C major, Hob. XVI. 10

EXERCISE 22.12   Figured Bass

Add upper voices to the figured basses below, each of which modulates by sequence.

A.

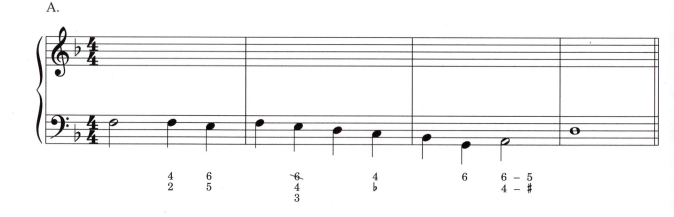

B.

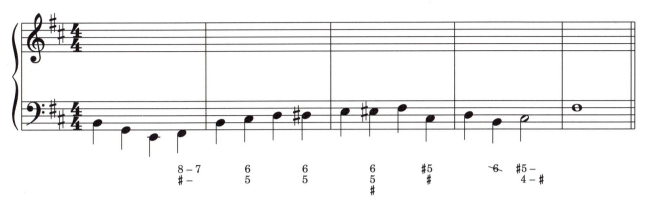

$$\begin{array}{ccccccc} 8-7 & 6 & 6 & 6 & \#5 & 6 & \#5- \\ \#- & 5 & 5 & 5 & \# & & 4-\# \\ & & & \# & & & \end{array}$$

EXERCISE 22.13   Writing Modulating Sequences

Complete the following ordered tasks.

A. Write a progression that

1. establishes F major.
2. incorporates a diatonic D2(D5/A4) sequence that breaks off early and becomes a pivot leading to the new key of vi.
3. establishes the key of vi.

B. Write a progression in C minor that modulates to III using an A2 (D3/A4) sequence; cadence in the new key.

C. Write a progression in B minor that modulates to iv using a D2 (D5/A4) sequence with applied chords; cadence in the new key.

D. Write a progression that

1. establishes A major using a descending bass arpeggiation.
2. modulates to iii using any sequence you wish.
3. establishes iii with a step-descent bass.
4. cadences in iii.

EXERCISE 22.14   Dictation: Variations of a Structural Progression

Study the model below, then listen to and notate the bass and soprano voices, and provide roman numerals for the following elaborations of the model. Modulations to closely related keys will occur. Label pivot chords.

Model A

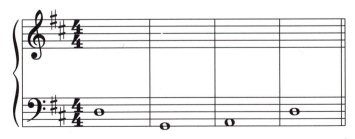

1.

2.

3.

4.

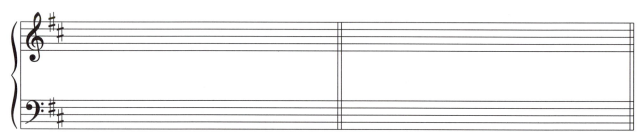

5.

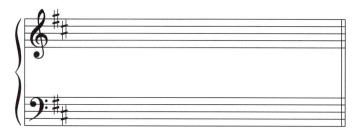

Model B

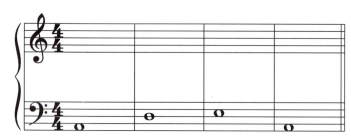

PD

1.

2.

3.

4.

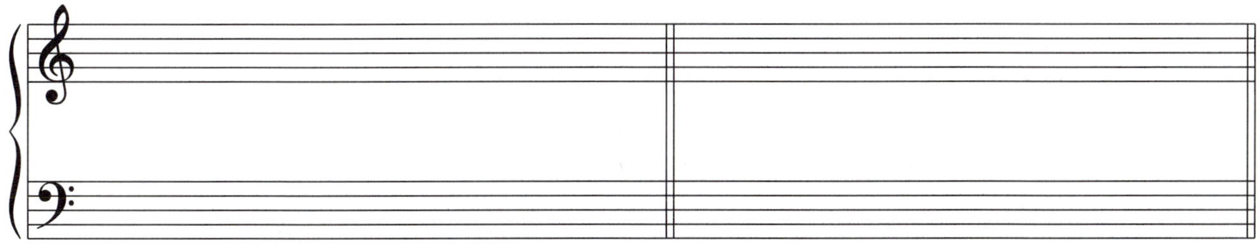

5.

Model C

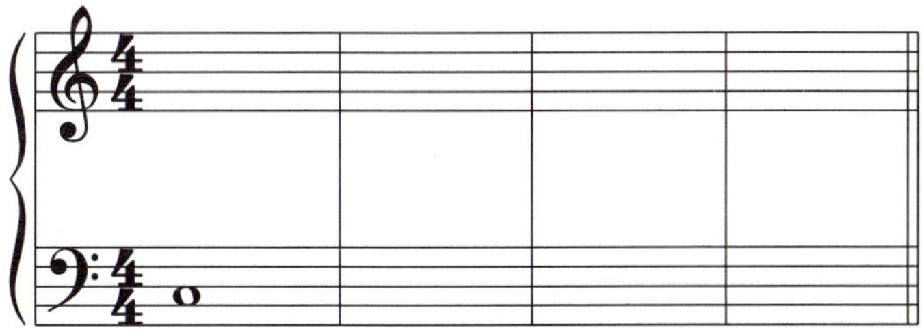

PD   V   I / i

1.

2.

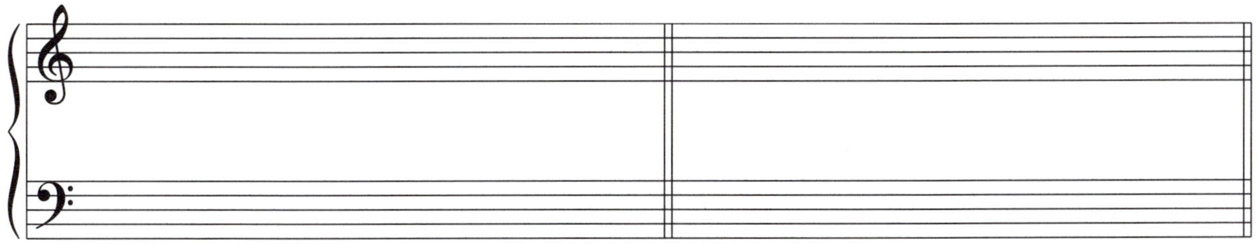

3.

4.

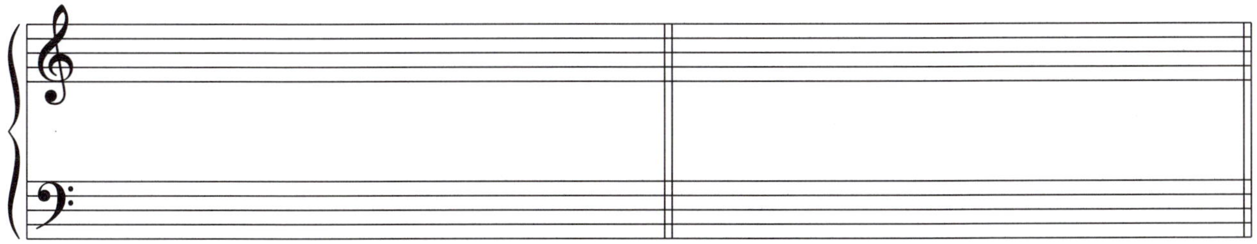

5.   6.

Model C

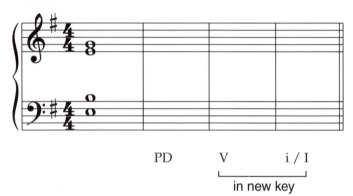

1.   2.

3.   4.

5.

EXERCISE 22.15   Composition

A.   Analyze the antecedent phrase below using roman numerals and figured bass; label tones of figuration and figured bass. Then, write three different consequent phrases to the antecedent, creating the following three period types: PIP, CIP, and PPP (you may close in either v or III).

B.   Analyze the chord progression in the first four measures of the example below. This will become the accompaniment for a melody that you will write. Then, in four voices, realize the figured bass that concludes the first phrase. Write a second phrase that modulates to and closes in a new key of your choice. Finally, write a suitable melody for both phrases.